THE LADY ACTRESS: RECOVERING THE LOST LEGACY OF A VICTORIAN AMERICAN SUPERSTAR

By Dr. Kelly S. Taylor

The Wapshott Press

THE LADY ACTRESS:
RECOVERING THE LOST LEGACY OF A
VICTORIAN AMERICAN SUPERSTAR

Published by
The Wapshott Press
An Imprint of J LHLS
PO Box 31513
Los Angeles, CA 90031
www.WapshottPress.com

First printing March 2009

Portions of this book have appeared in modified and edited
form in the following publications:

"Exploiting the Medium: Mesmerism and the Strange Case of
Anna Cora Mowatt." Text and Performance Quarterly 16:4,
(1996):321-335. (Peer Reviewed) (1.1b)

"The Creation of a Public Persona in the Poetry of Anna Cora
Mowatt." American Periodicals 11, (2001):65-80.

"Fear, Loathing, and Fashion: Self-Creation in the Comedy of
Anna Cora Mowatt." Theater Annual 54, (2001):43-61.

ISBN: 978-0-615-26250-5

06 05 04 03   4 3 2 1

Cover design by Kelly S. Taylor

Acknowledgements

As is usually true, a lot of people have had a hand in bringing this book to life. I'd like to take this opportunity to thank Dr. Mary Frances Hopkins of Louisiana State University for all the evenings she generously let me sit at her kitchen table and work through trouble spots in this manuscript while feeding me the most delicious pecan pralines ever to pass the lips of a mortal.

I'd like to thank my ex-husband John Taylor for the love, support, and space he gave me for writing – and for not dying of impatience before it was done.

Thanks to Dr. Ruth Bowman, Dr. Michael Bowman, Dr. Harold Mixon, and Dr. Gresna Doty to their invaluable input on this research project.

Thanks to the readers who gave insightful advice on tailoring this work to a non-academic audience. In particular, I want to thank Jane Seaton for seeing that each "i" was dotted and each "t" crossed.

Many thanks to Cindy Gordon and Karen Kimball for the excellent job they did in doing the final round of proofreading on this book.

Finally, I want to give an big, expansive, positively Victorian effusion of authorial gratitude to Ginger Mayerson for making my dream of finally publishing this little volume come true!

Table of Contents

CHAPTER 1

**FASHIONED LADY:
THE LIFE AND MANY CAREERS OF
ANNA CORA MOWATT**

Anna Cora Mowatt Ritchie, a mid-nineteenth century American author, public reader, playwright and actress, was a well-known and respected figure among her contemporaries in American literary and dramatic circles. Despite this, she is largely forgotten to modern theater lovers. In her day, she played to packed theaters and could number Edgar Allen Poe, David Henry Thoreau, and Ralph Waldo Emerson among her fans. Oral Interpretation scholars have called her the first "lady" elocutionist because she was the first female to enter the career of public reader without a previous career on the stage. In 1989, John Gentile, writing a history of prominent solo performers, credited her, along with famed actresses Fanny Kemble and Charlotte Cushman, with bringing to solo performance a level of prestige previously unknown in America. He claimed that they, as respectable women in a traditionally disrespected career, brought a respectability and an acceptance that allowed women of a later age to enjoy professional platform careers.[1] Her brief career as a public reader inspired many imitators.

Mowatt was also one of the first American women to achieve popular success as a playwright. Mrs. Mercy Warren, Charlotte Lennox and Susan Rowson were among her few forerunners. Her best remembered play, *Fashion*, was acclaimed by audiences and critics alike. The comedy frequently appears in contemporary anthologies of representative American dramas. Theater historians mark *Fashion* as one of the first successful efforts to create a distinctively American comedy of manners.[1] Following the success of *Fashion*, Mowatt reigned as one of the queens of American drama during her eight year acting career.

Off the stage, Mowatt played a wide range of roles—many of which would seem to contradict each other in light of the particular time, place, and social context of her life. She identified herself as both an actress and a respectable member of the American upper class. She worked outside her home to support herself and her husband, but still saw herself as a quite conventional wife and daughter.

Despite her radical career choices, it would be misleading to label Mowatt as a feminist. She was not sympathetic with the efforts of the early proponents of the Woman's Movement in America. She continually deferred to men and conventional middle-class values. However, when the conventional expectations of her peers would have made her a pariah, Anna Cora Mowatt rejected these perceived limitations. Through successfully creating and defending discursive authority for herself in her works, Mowatt won the freedom to assume social roles previously thought to be outside the definition of what it meant to be a proper upper-class lady in Victorian America.

For instance, many features of Mowatt's sociocultural context worked against a person who wanted to seek fame via a stage career and still wished to be perceived as a "lady." Mowatt's decision was shocking not only because it took her out of the womanly sphere of house and home, but because she was opting to go as a participant to a place where most "decent" people were uneasy about going even as spectators. Despite the respect and admiration given individual actors such as Fanny Kemble, Edmund Kean, and others, actors and actresses were generally viewed as low and common persons. After visiting America in the early part of the 19th century, English writer

Mrs. Trollope concluded that the general public in America did not approve of theatrical exhibitions. Her complaint about Cincinnati is typical of her comments about the few American cities where she found theaters:

> [Cincinnati has] a theater, which is, in fact, the only public amusement of this *triste* little town; but they seem to care little about it, and either from economy or distaste, it is very poorly attended. Ladies are rarely seen there, and by far the larger proportion of females deem it an offense against religion to witness the representation of a play. [2]
>
> Clara Morris, a 19th century American actress, wrote in her autobiography that "even the people who did not think all actors drunkards and all actresses immoral did think they were a lot of flighty, silly buffoons, not to be taken seriously for a moment." She went on to complain that although the cloud of public suspicion was beginning to lift by the 1860's, the individual actor "had no social standing." [3]

Not only was the vagabond lifestyle of actors suspect and their morality thought dubious at best, many believed that an actor or actress engaged in the art of mimesis at the peril of his/her own soul.

One minister wrote in 1827:

> The effect of the kind of life led by players is peculiarly pernicious to the female character. It strips it of all its loftier attributes, its softer and more delicate charms. Sensibility, modesty and refinement are gradually extinguished by the unfeminine and indelicate business of the stage and nothing is left but the hackneyed and haggard form of injured humanity,

covered and bedecked perhaps, by false and tawdry ornaments. A few female actors may have preserved their virtue, but alas! how many have lost it forever by their connection with the stage. And if others have not been entirely ruined by this means, how greatly must their character have suffered in purity and elevation, by the dark forms of evil with which they come into such close and continual contact.[4]

The stage was condemned from the pulpit and shunned by many respectable persons.[5] With the exception of the Episcopal Church, virtually every Protestant sect in America officially and unequivocally declared the theater the haunt of sinners.[6] Moreover, religious leaders even promoted a belief that mere association with actors and actresses was morally injurious. Reverend Robert Hatfield rhetorically asked his flock, "Let me ask you, my young friend, justly proud of your sister, would you rather not follow her to her grave tonight than to know that tomorrow she shall stand at the altar and pledge her faith and trust her precious future to an actor?"[7] Reverend Thomas DeWitt Talmadge, pastor of the largest congregation in New York during the 1870's, declared that most people would rather see their children "five feet under the ground of Greenwood" than "in a month's association with actors."[8]

Although it is difficult to document how widely the general public shared the views promoted by many churches, it is clear that theatrical professionals believed the populace was inclined against them. American actor John Hodginson wrote in his 1797 autobiography of "strong and widely held prejudices" against the profession.[9] Successful theatrical managers William Wood, Sol Smith, and Noah Ludlow, all complained bitterly about the church's antipathy towards theater and indicated its destructive effect on the profession.[10]   Albert A. Palmer, a successful theater owner and manager, wrote in 1895 that by his estimate at least seven-tenths of the population in mid-century still looked on theater attendance as "almost a sin."[11]

In advice he dispensed in his July 19, 1845, review of Mowatt's acting debut at the Park Theater, Edgar Allan Poe warned Mowatt of dangers to her reputation. He perceived that certain choices she made concerning the scheduling of her debut could harm her standing in the theatrical community:

> She has erred, we think, in making this arrangement—that is to say, she has somewhat injured the prestige of her name, first appearing at a summer theater, and secondly in appearing again after so brief an interval. Mrs. Mowatt owes it to herself to maintain a certain dignity; and, although this certain dignity be preposterous, in fact in the fiction of the world's view it is all important. A lady so well-connected, and so well established in the public eye by her literary career, could have had no difficulty in coming upon the stage in her own fashion, and almost on her own terms. The Park, as the place of her debut, was, of course, unobjectionable, although in a negative sense. She lost no caste by coming out here, but the fact cannot be disputed that she would have gained much by first appearing in London, and presenting herself to her country men and country women with the eclat of a foreign reputation. We say this, with a bitter sense of our national degradation, and subserviency to British opinion—we say it, moreover, with a consciousness that Mrs. Mowatt should not have done this thing however much it

would have furthered her interests.[12]

Even among actors, Poe implied, there were degrees of respectability that Mowatt needed to take into consideration.

In the same article he went on to refute the anti-theatrical prejudice he noted among his peers:

We have no sympathies with the prejudices which would entirely have dissuaded Mrs. Mowatt from the stage. There is no cant more contemptible than that which habitually decries the theatrical profession - a profession, which, in itself, embraces all that can elevate and ennoble, and absolutely nothing to degrade. If some—if many—or if nearly all of its members are dissolute, this is an evil arising not from the profession itself, but from the unhappy circumstances which surround it. With these circumstances Mrs. Mowatt has, at present, no concern. With talents, enthusiasm, and energy, she will both honor the stage and derive from it honor. In the mere name of actress she can surely find nothing to dread - nothing, or she would be unworthy of the profession - not the profession unworthy of her. The theater is ennobled by its high facilities for the development of genius—facilities not afforded elsewhere in equal degree. By the spirit of genius, we say, it is ennobled—it is sanctified—beyond the sneer of the fool or the cant of the hypocrite.[13]

Although as the son of actors, Poe was not an unbiased observer, he, too, noted and decried the lack of regard for actors he saw demonstrated by his peers.

In addition to contemporary feeling against theater, many Victorians seemed, as Leslie Hume and Karen Offen stated in *Victorian Women*, reluctant to accept women who did any sort of work outside the home:

As that gospel [of work] concerned women, however, it had a narrow application. Victorian prescriptive literature celebrated women's work in the home and applauded the notion of good household management. But authors of those texts—many of whom were women—did not acknowledge, much less celebrate, women's work outside the domestic sphere. In fact, they promoted an ideology of domesticity that perpetuated the notion that the only appropriate working activities for women were domestic tasks. Like the French historian Jules Michelet, they believed that the term *ouvriere* (working woman) was an "impiety," an outrage.[14]

Although an estimated 9.7% of American women worked in 1870, making up 14.8% of the total working population, the working woman was still a questionable figure.[15]

No one forbade American women of the pre-Civil War period to write and publish poems, novels, non-fiction or even plays. A good number of women did and made a respectable amount of money for their efforts. However, many people were not entirely at ease with the idea of women writers. In a letter to his publisher William Ticknor in January of 1855, Nathaniel Hawthorne referred to them as a "d—d mob of scribbling women."[16] The reputedly 'gentle-hearted' Charles Lamb said of English poetess Letitia Elizabeth Landon in 1854, "If she belonged to me, I would lock her up on bread and water till she left off writing poetry. A female poet, or female author of any kind, ranks below an actress, I think."[17]

In entering the marketplace as writers, women were trespassing into economic as well as intellectual territory traditionally held by men. Many like Hawthorne feared that "the ink-stained Amazons will expel their rivals by actual pressure, and petticoats wave triumphantly over all the field."[18] Although women could walk onto the playing field of the literary market in the early nineteenth century, they had to step carefully in order to avoid male ire and/or being labeled unfeminine. Sarah Josepha Hale cautioned aspiring poetesses in her <u>Lady's Magazine</u> (a precursor to <u>Godey's Lady's Book</u>):

> The path of poetry, like every other path in life, is
> to the tread of women, exceedingly circumscribed.
> She may not revel in the luxuriance of fancies, images
> and thoughts, or indulge in the license of choosing
> themes at will, like the Lords of creation.[19]

Sara Clarke, a popular authoress who published under the pseudonym "Grace Greenwood," wrote in the preface to Greenwood Leaves that "true feminine genius is ever timid, doubtful, and clingingly dependent; a perpetual childhood. A true woman shrinks from greatness." She cautioned other would-be female writers that the true joys of creativity were, "for the masters of the lyre; it can never be felt by women with great intensity; at least, can never satisfy her."[20] Female authors, no matter how successful, were characteristically reluctant to take credit for their own creations. Harriet Beecher Stowe announced that "God wrote" *Uncle Tom's Cabin*. Susan Warner's sister explained that Warner had written her sentimental bestseller *The Wide, Wide World* (published in 1850) "in close reliance upon God; for thoughts, for power and for words... In that sense, the book was written on her knees."[21] Catharine Maria Sedgwick claimed that when writing she was "but the instrument of God."[22] Because of the challenge it presented to male authority, while not forbidden, the role of woman writer was not a comfortable one.

Anna Cora Mowatt was able to establish discursive authority in the face of such social sanctions because she actively exercised (and even today posthumously exercises) control over the interpretation of her actions. Mowatt was, in the language of modern public relations experts, her own best "spin doctor." Much that we know of Mowatt comes from her own autobiography. In this work, and all the other modes of public expression Mowatt used—non-fiction, fiction, performance, plays, and poetry—she employed potent rhetorical strategies to present herself, her desires, and her motivations in a way that would mitigate the effects of her society's prejudices without alienating her auditors.

In her introduction to *Fictions of Authority*, Susan Lanser states that before anyone can speak with true authority about woman writers and the strategies they employ to establish an authoritative voice, many more studies of women's texts from many different cultures and from many different vantage points must be done.[23] Anna Cora Mowatt was a white, Western, upper-class woman like Jane Austen, George Eliot, Charlotte Bronte and others that Lanser profiles in her book. However, looking at Mowatt's life and various works has given me, as a researcher, the opportunity to examine a woman's attempts to establish discursive authority in many creative forms other than just the novel. Anna Cora Ogden Mowatt Ritchie was a lady who lived up to the complexity and variety of her elaborate composite name. A Renaissance woman of the Victorian era, she achieved popular and critical success in an impressively wide range of creative outlets. She was also successful in her quest to create through rhetorical/textual strategies an authoritative voice in her varied works. In these works, Mowatt fashioned a public voice for herself without appearing to her auditors to be a cunning, manipulative, usurper of masculine power.

I have chosen to refer to Anna Cora Ogden Mowatt Ritchie throughout this study as Anna Cora Mowatt. After her second marriage, she dropped Mowatt and adopted her husband's surname. However, since she achieved fame as an actress, playwright, author, and public reader as Mowatt, contemporary references use that name. To avoid confusion, I have decided to refer to her consistently as Mowatt rather than switching back and forth or using Mowatt-Ritchie as she never did.

Mowatt's life was a process of constant negotiation. Although she did enjoy the privileges of class, as a woman and an actress, she was often outside spheres of power in her culture. As Susan Lanser points out in *Fictions of Authority*, social identity is linked to narrative form. The authority of a given voice or text is produced from a conjunction of social and rhetorical practices. What Lanser calls discursive authority, or the intellectual credibility, ideological validity, and aesthetic value claimed by or conferred upon a work, author, narrator or textual practice, is produced interactively with specific receiving communities.[24] As Lanser states, discursive authority in mid-nineteenth century was most readily available to white, educated men of hegemonic ideology.[25] However, because narrative authority is also constituted through textual/rhetorical strategies that even socially unauthorized voices may appropriate, Mowatt, despite her gender and her profession, had the opportunity to fight for an authoritative public voice. As a nonhegemonic writer she had to, as Lanser emphasizes, "strike a delicate balance in accommodating and subverting the status quo."[26] This book is an inquiry into Anna Cora Mowatt's quest to fashion a self who could speak with an authoritative public voice. I devote a chapter to a sample of each genre of public expression Mowatt used: nonfiction, fiction, performance, play-writing, and poetry.

I have allowed myself the luxury of choosing several texts for examination that have an obvious autobiographical bent. However, I think it would be equally possible and profitable for a researcher to take the same approach to any other works by Mowatt. The author carefully creates a public persona in her anonymous articles on housekeeping and *Life of Goethe*, (the only work she wrote under a male pseudonym) just as she does in her autobiography. The novels *Evelyn* and *The Mute Singer* contain ideas that gently contradict popular beliefs just as *Mimic Life* does. An examination of Mowatt's successful portrayal of numerous beloved ingénues could be as productive as my look at her private experimentation with mesmerism. The play *Armand* says as much about its time as does *Fashion*. "On a Lock of My Mother's Hair" or the verse play *Pelayo* provide fields of study as rich as the poem "My Life." In short,

I did not set out to exhaust Mowatt and her works as a subject for study.

From her body of non-fictive writing, I have chosen to look at her autobiography. Mowatt was able to get around the difficulties of writing as a woman in the first person when writing her autobiography by giving solid, believable, acceptable reasons for writing, and for creating a writing persona that appeared frank, candid, and genuinely humble. In this non-fictive work, Mowatt wooed her suspicious public by fashioning an implied self that was not proud, self-aggrandizing, or threateningly unfeminine. She created a narrative voice that readers could feel comfortable indulging with their attention while crafting a narrative framework for her life story that was familiar to her auditors. In the absence of an appropriate pattern for women's life stories, Mowatt borrowed from popular fiction and skillfully employed narrative devices that enhanced her credibility as a speaker by underplaying the aggressive unconventionality of her life story.

Mimic Life extends the work Mowatt started in her autobiography in fictive form. Mowatt employed the authoritative public voice that she had so carefully created in her non-fictional account of her life to carry on her fight against the anti-theatrical prejudice she found among her peers. Through the creation of sympathetic characters and narratives filled with pathos, she attempted to turn the tide of contempt and disrespect in which she believed many conventional Victorians held the theater and its workers.

Although Mowatt was well-known and well-loved for her work on the public stage, as an example of her performance work I choose to look at a form of private theatrical. Mesmerism was a stage where upper class Victorians could ignore temporarily the strict social rules for their social strata and perform experiments testing their social/cultural beliefs. Working with her mesmerizers, Mowatt created an alternate persona that called herself "the Gypsy." In a way that the many true-hearted but hopelessly conventional maidens Anna Cora played before the public never could, the Gypsy voiced Mowatt's private dissatisfactions. The unreal Gypsy was free within the experimental context of mesmeric sessions to give vent to the full range of Mowatt's intelligence, aggression, and rebellion. Mowatt was never given the opportunity as an actress or in her own life to play a character as openly confrontational as the Gypsy.

Mowatt's hit comedy *Fashion* accurately tapped into a myriad of nagging fears and anxieties in her audience about the growing artificiality of interaction in urban life. Her unexpectedly masterful demonstration of narrative skill in creating the play promoted a vision of herself as the implied author that was worthy of her auditors' attention and admiration. This implied author was worldly enough to court both liberals and conservatives, while at the same time successfully walking the narrow line between satirizing and offending her own social class. Since the subject of the play was the appropriately feminine topic of "fashion," however, Mowatt's potentially unladylike expertise did not alarm her auditors.

Finally, Mowatt, like most "literary ladies" of her day, tried on the role of poetess for size. The lady poet, unlike the lady playwright or lady novelist, trespassed to a lesser degree onto what was culturally considered male literary territory. As Mowatt vigorously attempted to do in her forays into other artistic fields, the poetess could express herself publicly without automatically sacrificing her position as a lady. The metaphor-laden, ambiguous language common in women's poetry of this Post-Romantic age allowed the poetess to express deep feelings without necessarily making her social criticisms sharp or revealing many hard facts about herself.

Mowatt played both the rebel and the conservative in her time. By keeping her unconventionality carefully concealed by narrative and rhetorical acumen, Mowatt was able to have her cultural cake and eat it too. She was an independent working woman in a time when, as Hume and Offen attest, upper and middle class writers and speakers often looked on such women with suspicion or scorn.[58] She presented herself to the public in the questionable roles of actress and lady author and still managed to pull off the feat of being generally acclaimed a lady.

CHAPTER 2

A RADIANTLY BEAUTIFUL SMILE:
A BRIEF HISTORY OF ANNA CORA MOWATT

Anna Cora Ogden Mowatt Ritchie was born in Bordeaux, France, March 5, 1819. She was the tenth of the fourteen children of Eliza Lewis and Samuel Gouveneur Ogden. Ogden (1779-1860), a New York merchant who was peripherally involved in the failed effort of Venezuelan patriot Francisco de Miranda to liberate South American from Spanish rule,[1] was at the time of Anna Cora's birth residing in France to act as an agent for foreign exporters. Eliza Lewis Ogden (1785-1836) was the granddaughter of Declaration of Independence signer Francis Lewis.[2] In accordance with French law, Anna Cora and three of her sisters became French citizens shortly after their birth.[3]

The Ogden family returned to America in 1826 on the ship *Brandt* when Anna Cora was six years old. The boat was wrecked by a storm. One of her brothers was lost at sea in this storm. Anna Cora claimed that the respiratory problems that were to plague her for the rest of her life started as a result of her prolonged exposure to the elements while the family awaited rescue.[4]

She was interested in the stage even as a child of five. Anna Cora played her first role that year, appearing as a judge (with no lines to speak) in a production of *Othello* that her older brothers and sisters put on for her parents in their home. She wrote poetry from an early age and read all of Shakespeare's plays before she was ten. When she was fourteen, she staged and starred in a translation of Voltaire's *Alzire* in her Flatbush home.

Anna Cora attended several private schools in New York in addition to instruction by tutors at home. By far her most ardent teacher was James Mowatt (1805-1849). Mowatt, a prosperous New York lawyer, had originally come to the Ogden household as a suitor of Anna Cora's older sister Charlotte. His interest turned to fourteen-year-old Anna Cora. He became a frequent visitor and took over the direction of Anna Cora's education, creating reading lists for her and discussing the books she read. In 1834, one year before Anna Cora was to debut in New York society, Mowatt persuaded her to elope with him. They were married on October 6, 1834, by a French minister who performed the ceremony in French. James Mowatt was twenty-eight years old and Anna Cora was only fifteen. Anna Cora wrote of her elopement:

> What could a girl of fifteen know of the sacred duties of a wife? With what eyes could she comprehend the new and important life she was entering? She had known nothing but childhood—had scarcely commenced her girlhood. What could she comprehend of the trials, the cares, the hopes, the responsibilities of womanhood? I thought of none of these things. I had always been lighthearted to the point of frivolity. I usually made a jest of everything—yet I did not look on this matter as a frolic. I only remembered I was keeping a promise. I had perfect faith in the tenderness of him to whom I confided myself. I did not in the least realize the novelty of my situation.[5]

The Mowatts had no children. One biographical sketch

characterizes James Mowatt as "more like a doting father than a husband."[6]

After their marriage, Mowatt purchased a pre-revolutionary mansion located on a twenty-acre country estate in Flatbush, Long Island. The couple named the estate Melrose. James Mowatt played the role of instructor to his child wife. He continued Anna Cora's studies in English, French, Spanish and music. A journal of critiques and comments she kept at the time indicates she read between ninety and one hundred books yearly under his direction.[7]

Mowatt published a historical romance in verse that Anna Cora had written at age seventeen using the pseudonym "Isabel." The title was *Pelayo, or The Cavern of Covadonga* (1837). Inspired by Schlegel's "Lectures on Literature," Anna Cora decided to write an epic poem. *Pelayo* is a poetical romance in six cantos, based on the history of the successor of Roderick the Goth, who in 718 was chosen the first king of the Asturias. The poem shows influences of Byron, Southey, and Halleck.

In her preface, Anna Cora pleaded for the indulgence of her critics:

> In this "Golden Age," (or age of gold) I should indeed be presumptuous to suppose such "unprofitable stuff" as rhymes could ever be vendable—unless, indeed, with patched robe of many hues, and killing Gipsy bonnet, I myself went singing them about the streets; for, you see, I have not even afforded gilt edges to make the pill go down;—but—if it will enhance their humble value, be it known to those that take interest in them, that both Dedication and Tale were written and finished before Isabel had completed her seventeenth year; and the only hasty revision they ever had, previous to being put in the printer's hands,

was immediately after. —I am as conscious of their innumerable faults as the severest judge could be; yet those who look with lenient eyes may again hear from Isabel.[8]

Incensed at the unfavorable notices from newspaper critics that appeared despite her plea and prompted by Byron's "English Bards and Scotch Reviewers," Anna Cora wrote (still using a pseudonym) a verse response entitled *Reviewers Reviewed*, which James Mowatt also had published in 1837. In this poem, she creates a fictive Court of Justice where the spirits of Justice, Prudence, Ambition, and Truth try critics George P. Morris (of the *New York Mirror*), James Watson Webb and Mr. Daniels (of the *Courier and Enquirer*), Colonel Stone (of the *Commercial Advertiser*), and Lewis Gaylord Clark (of the *Knickerbocker*). At one point she compares Mr. Webb to a spider:

> Welcome, all-conquering Webb! that gossamer name,
> Remembereth well thy even lighter frame–
> Thy snare-deceiving self, and wily creed–
> For, webs catch foolish flies—and spiders feed
> On hapless victims to their arts decreed;
> Th' unwary thus are lured within thy toils,
> While even spider-like thou'lt seize the spoils.
>
> So shalt thou—as a thing that fame knows not,
> Like a spider live—like a spider die forgot!
> We hail thee King, Great Webb! of all the mob!
> Long life! and should thy subjects chance to rob
> That purse which by such honest means was filled,
> Ay, prithee—let some character be killed.
> The world loves slander, and thy blanket sheet
> Shall soon with new subscriptions be replete.[9]

I agree with other commentators who have noted that although by no means a great poem, *Reviewers Reviewed* is a far more passionate and original piece of writing than the work it defends.[10]

At this time, Anna Cora developed symptoms of tuberculosis. Believing a change of climate would provide relief, the Mowatts scheduled a sea voyage to Europe. They lived abroad for nearly three years. During this time Anna Cora took German and voice lessons from a singing teacher. She also witnessed performances by two of the most famous and respected actresses of that day: Madame Vestris and her troupe in London and the great tragedian Rachel in Paris. Anna Cora later submitted articles based on her European experiences and observations to several American periodicals. "Bridal Customs of the Northern Germans" was published in *The Ladies' Companion* (edited by Sarah Josepha Hale), July, 1841, and "Usages and Manners of the North Germans" appeared in the October, 1841, issue of the same magazine. "A Bridal in Germany" and "Dancing Among the Germans" both appeared in Epes Sargent's *Sargent's Magazine* in May and April of 1843.

While in France, James Mowatt developed an eye ailment that effectively blinded him for four months. To amuse herself during his confinement, Anna Cora wrote a six-act play entitled *Gulzara, or the Persian Slave*. The play was designed for an all-female cast consisting of herself and three of her younger sisters. She planned to perform *Gulzara* at a grand ball celebrating the Mowatts' return to New York. Anna Cora commissioned a prominent French scene painter to create six backdrops, one for each act.[11]

Gulzara, the Persian slave of the title, is captured by the men of Sultan Suliman for the Sultan's harem. She longs to return to Hafed, the man with whom she is in love. Ayesha, the wife of the fisherman Rustapha, has been ill-treated by the sultan. During the ruler's absence, she retaliates by kidnapping his son, Ammarth. Gulzara is accused of the crime and thrown into prison. In the meantime, the sultan sends a letter home saying he has been victorious in battle and is returning to marry Gulzara. The sultan, when he returns, turns out to be Gulzara's lover, Hafed.

Gulzara was presented by Mrs. Mowatt and her sisters at Melrose on October 17, 1840. A large circle of friends from New York's social elite attended. In the audience was Epes Sargent (1813-1880), associate editor of *The New World* (New York). He was so impressed by the play—and Anna Cora—that he printed the entire script of *Gulzara* in that paper. Editor Park Benjamin wrote the following to introduce the script:

> We have the pleasure of announcing for publication in the next New World an original drama in five acts by Mrs. James Mowatt of N.Y. It is entitled "Gulzara, or the Persian Slave"; and we think the reader will concede it displays dramatic and poetical abilities of no ordinary power. This drama, though never publicly represented, was performed last winter before a select circle of friends in excellent style and with most flattering success. We do not doubt it will be eagerly sought for by the friends of our native literature. The story is extremely interesting, and the style is rich, flowing and replete with beauties.[12]

Gulzara was the first of Anna Cora Mowatt's works to appear under her own name.

Continued degeneration of his eyesight forced James Mowatt to abandon his law practice. He briefly entered into a partnership in a publishing firm. Anna Cora published several works with this firm including a biography of Goethe (written under the pseudonym Henry C. Browning) and two novels *The*

Fortune Hunter; or, The Adventures of a Man about Town and *Evelyn; or, A Heart Unmasked* (both published under the name Helen Berkeley).

The Fortune Hunter won a $100 prize in a contest sponsored by *The New World*. The book achieved extensive sales, a number of editions, and translation into German. The novel tells the story of Augustus Brainard, who having spent his fortune, is introduced into New York society by Ellery, a "man about town," who hopes to help his friend to make a profitable marriage. At one point Ellery advises Augustus that Niblo's is unquestionably the place to go since

> ...all the fashionables will be there, and so will all the good religious people who think the theater (where Shakespere's noble drama is represented) a shocking place—but look upon Niblo's little stage, his vaudevilles and rope-dancers as perfectly proper.[13]

The Fortune Hunter is an attempt at satire upon New York society and romantic sentimentalism, a theme that Anna Cora would later develop further in *Fashion*.

Evelyn is a multi-volume domestic narrative told in epistolary style. The plot hinges on the desire of Mr. and Mrs. Willard to marry their daughter Evelyn to a rich man so they can all live in luxury. Their scheme ends in tragedy. Mowatt added a strong dose of social satire to Evelyn's melodrama. Take, for example, one character's description of Mr. Willard:

> As far as I can judge of ages, Mr. Willard must be about forty. Picture to yourself a taciturn individual, who never speaks beyond a common-place, and yet delivers his remarks with as much impressive gravity as though he considered every sentence an aphorism. In person tall and gaunt, with arms and legs which are

a dreadful encumbrance to him, for he never knows
what to do with them—a thin and sallow face, but
features too heavy to be sharp, in spite of the
projecting cheek-bones and hollow cheeks—small,
round, grey eyes—over hanging brows furnished with
a goodly quantity of reddish hair—a consumptive pair
of whiskers of deep auburn hue, curtailed in an even
line from the mouth—a low and deeply furrowed
forehead—thin, compressed lips, through which the
shape of horse-like teeth is partially visible—a
habitual frown, that denotes calculation, care and
disappointment—picture all these, and you will see
Mr. Willard, with folded arms and a very absorbed
mien sitting before you... [He] is a Wall-Street broker,
but as he never had anything to lose—not even
credit—the most ruinous speculation cannot harm
him.[14]

The novel gives a snapshot of New York life in the 1840's.
In its pages one learns, for example, that adults of that decade
loved to play games like battledore and shuttlecock and give
tableaux. They took tamarind water for fevers. They politely
placed coffins in vacant apartments so that any outsider could
view the corpse. New York was at this time the only city where
railroad cars and omnibuses were patronized by "the wealthiest
and most exclusive classes as well as the less affluent."[15]

Despite the success of Anna Cora's novels and her other
shorter works, the Mowatts' publishing venture failed. James
Mowatt also lost great amounts speculating on real estate. The
strict enforcement of President Jackson's financial reforms
caused a sudden state of bankruptcy for Mowatt. When it
seemed certain that the Mowatts were to lose Melrose, Anna
Cora decided to utilize her dramatic talents to help stabilize the
couple's financial situation. Although she was apparently not
bold enough to leap directly from the role of society matron to

the profession of actress, she decided to give a series of public readings in the style of Fanny Kemble and American actor and elocutionist George Vanderhoff.

After seeking and receiving consent to do so from her father and husband, she scheduled her first readings at the Masonic Temple in Boston, home of her good friend Epes Sargent. When she stepped on the stage of the Tremont Street Temple Place on Thursday, October 28, 1841, she became the first female to enter the career of public reader without a previous career on the stage. Her success spawned a small army of imitators.

Her readings included selections from Sir Walter Scott, Mrs. Felicia Hemans, Oliver Wendell Homes, Thomas Campbell, Lord Byron, Thomas More, and Samuel Taylor Coleridge. She also read "The Missing Ship," a sensational poem about the mysterious disappearance at sea of the steamship *President*, written especially for her by Epes Sargent. In Providence, one woman was so affected by Anna Cora's reading of this particular poem that she had to be carried from the hall in a fit of hysterics.[15]

Edgar Allan Poe, who attended readings she gave in New York, described Anna Cora:

> Her figure is slight, even fragile. Her face is a remarkably fine one, and of that precise character best adapted to the stage. The forehead is, perhaps, the least prepossessing feature, although it is by no means an unintellectual one. Hair light auburn, in rich profusion, and always arranged with exquisite taste. The eyes are gray, brilliant, and expressive, without being full. The nose is well formed, with the Roman curve, and indicative of energy. This quality is also shown in the somewhat excessive prominence of the chin. The mouth is large, with brilliant and even teeth

and flexible lips, capable of the most instantaneous and effective variation of expression. A more radiantly beautiful smile is quite impossible to conceive.[16]

The public readings were a critical and popular success, although some felt the success was largely due to Mrs. Mowatt's "radiantly beautiful smile." A percentage of her friends and family from New York's upper crust were shocked at her decision to exhibit herself in such a fashion. Several openly snubbed her.[17] The readings also failed to solve the Mowatts' financial difficulties. The Mowatts sold Melrose and moved into apartments in the Astor House in 1842.

Anna Cora developed severe respiratory problems and abruptly ended her career as a public reader. She was an invalid for the better part of the next four years. In her autobiography, she reports that she began a series of mesmeric treatments from Dr. William Francis Channing at this time; however, letters by Epes Sargent in 1842 indicate that she was already under Dr. Channing's care while still engaged in public readings.[18]

Mowatt devotes an entire chapter of her autobiography to a description of the unusual cure she underwent. Epes Sargent echoes her account in his *The Scientific Basis of Spiritualism* published in 1881. According to Mowatt and Sargent, mesmerism not only relieved Anna Cora's respiratory symptoms but elevated her to a higher state of consciousness where she could do all sorts of incredible things. She could write and embroider in absolute darkness, predict crises in her illness in advance, diagnose illnesses in others, and remain insensible to pain. Mowatt, under mesmeric influence, developed a second personality who called herself the "Gypsy" and Mowatt's waking self the "little Fool." The Gypsy wrote many poems and stories and loved to debate philosophy and religion for hours with Sargent and James Mowatt. Sargent wrote of her:

> It is rare that a subject reaches the high stage to which she has attained. In her case we see daily proved the most ultra and incredible facts reported of magnetism—facts, which we dare not tell her in her waking state nor anyone else—so let nothing of this be intimated. This I will tell you, however, as one of the least remarkable. I have conversed mentally with her for several minutes—she replying vocally to my unuttered questions, and sometimes even anticipating my thoughts by placing her hand on my head.[19]

During these mesmeric experiences, Anna Cora and James Mowatt converted to the New Church, following the teachings of Emmanuel Swedenborg, the Swedish visionary. Anna Cora reports that James was converted to Swedenborgism from his discussions with the Gypsy. He, in turn, encouraged Anna Cora to study this new religion of which she claimed to have no previous knowledge in her waking state.[20]

During her convalescence she began work on a five act comedy called *Fashion; or, Life in New York*. She did so at the recommendation of Sargent, who suggested that the comedy would be "a fresh channel for the sarcastic ebullitions with which you so constantly indulge us."[21] The play was a keen but good-natured satire on American parvenuism. She presented the New York social scene in all its pretense and gullibility, its tendency to ape Parisian customs, and its exaltation of money.

Mrs. Tiffany, the wife of a newly rich business man, has high social ambitions for herself and her daughter Seraphina. Her extravagance is ruining her husband, who is caught in financial misconduct by his clerk Snobson, who proceeds to blackmail him. Count Jolimaitre, who turns out to be actually a valet posing as a nobleman, is also after the Tiffanys' money.

The plot grows progressively thicker as the story unfolds. The source of *Fashion's* comedy is its satirizing of social pretensions as in the following scene between Mrs. Tiffany and her French maid, Millinette:

Mrs. Tiff.: Is everything in order, Millinette? Ah! very elegant, very elegant, indeed! There is a jenny-says quoi look about this furniture—an air of fashion and gentility perfectly bewitching. Is there not, Millinette?

Mil.: Oh, oui, Madame!

Mrs. Tif.: But where is Seraphina? It is twelve o'clock; our visitors will be pouring in, and she has not made her appearance. But I hear that nothing is more fashionable than to keep people waiting. None but vulgar persons pay any attention to punctuality. Is it not so, Millinette?

Mil.: Quite *comme il faut*. Great *personnes* always do make little *personnes* wait, Madame.

Mrs. Tif.: This mode of receiving visitors only upon one specified day of the week is a most convenient custom! It saves the trouble of keeping the house continually in order and of being always dressed. I flatter myself that I was the first to introduce it amongst the New York ee-light. You are quite sure that it is strictly a Parisian mode, Millinette?

Mil.: Oh, oui, Madame; entirely *mode de Paris*.

Mrs. Tif.: This girl is worth her weight in gold. (Aside.) Millinette, how do you say arm-chair in French?

Mil.: *Fauteuil*, Madame.

Mrs. Tif.: Fo-tool! That has a foreign, an out-the-wayish sound that is perfectly charming—and so genteel! There is something about our American words that is decidedly vulgar. Fowtool! how refined. Fow-tool! Arm-chair! what a difference!

Mil.: Madame have one *charmante* pronunciation. Fowtool (mimicking aside) *charmante*, Madame!

Mrs. Tif.: Do you think so, Millinette? Well, I believe I have. But a woman of refinement and of fashion can always accommodate herself to anything foreign! And a week's study of that invaluable work—"French without a Master," has made me quite at home with the court language of Europe! But where is the new valet? I'm rather sorry that he is black, but to obtain a white American domestic is almost impossible; and they call this a free country![22]

Fashion opened at the Park Theater, New York, on March 24, 1845. It was a great popular success and was generally well received by the critics. Edgar Allan Poe, writing for the *Broadway Journal*, felt the play derivative of *School for Scandal*, but notable for its genuinely American humor.[23]

Following the play's success, Anna Cora Mowatt, in a

complete reversal of her earlier distaste for the stage, appeared for the first time as an actress at the Park Theater, June 13, 1845. Her debut role was Pauline in the popular melodrama *Lady of Lyons*. For the next eight years, she became one of the foremost popular and critically acclaimed American actresses. She specialized in ingénue roles from Shakespeare, popular melodramas, and her own plays *Fashion* and *Armand*. Poe described her onstage appearance:

> The great charm of her manner is its naturalness. She looks, speaks, and moves, with a well-controlled impulsiveness, as different as can be conceived from the customary rant and cant, the hack conventionality of the stage. Her voice is rich and voluminous, and although by no means powerful, is so well managed as to seem so. Her utterance is singularly distinct, its sole blemish being the occasional Anglicism of accent, adopted probably from her instructor, Mr. Crisp. Her reading could scarcely be improved. Her action is distinguished by an ease and self-possession which would do credit to a veteran. Her step is the perfection of grace. Often have I watched her for hours with the closest scrutiny, yet never for an instant did I observe her in an attitude of the least awkwardness or even constraint, while many of her seemingly impulsive gestures spoke in loud terms of the woman of genius, of the poet imbued with the profoundest sentiment of the beautiful in motion.[24]

Actor E.L. Davenport joined Mowatt as acting partner in September of 1846. Mowatt wrote her second play, *Armand, the Child of the People*, with his and her capabilities in mind. *Armand* is a romantic play set in the time of Louis XV. The King tries to seduce Blanche, the daughter of the Duke of Richelieu. Armand, a soldier, falls in love with Blanche and strives to help her escape the king. Armand's defiance of the King, while hardly in keeping with the customs of the court of Louis XV, was quite in tone with the sentiments of America in 1847.

In 1847, Davenport and Mowatt sailed for London, where they achieved great popular and critical success. However, her English career came to an abrupt halt when James Mowatt died on February 15, 1851. She might have remained in England after her husband's death, but following this tragedy, her London manager, who was in love with her, went bankrupt and committed suicide. Depressed, dispirited, and ill with another recurrence of her respiratory condition, Mowatt returned to America in July, 1851.

After recovering, she resumed touring American theaters with productions of Fashion and Shakespearean comedies. During this time, she was vigorously pursued and courted by William Foushee Ritchie, son of Thomas Ritchie and editor of the Richmond Enquirer, the official organ of the Democratic Party in Virginia. In December of 1853, Mowatt published her *Autobiography of an Actress*. On June 3, 1854, she made her last appearance on the public stage. On June 7, 1853, she married William Foushee Ritchie in an elaborate Richmond wedding. Two thousand invitations were issued. Among the invited guests were the President of the United States (Franklin Pierce), his cabinet, and a large number of the members of the Congress and of the Virginia Legislature.[25]

During her years of marriage to Ritchie, Anna Cora became involved in the movement to preserve George Washington's home at Mount Vernon as a national historic site. She also wrote two fictional novels based on her experiences in the theater. *Mimic Life; or, Before and Behind the Curtain* (actually three novellas collected in one volume) was published in 1855 and *Twin Roses; a Narrative* in 1857.

Mimic Life is Mowatt's autobiography in fictional form. The first story, "Stella," parallels Mowatt's own debut as an actress. Other incidents in "The Unknown Tragedian" and "The Prompter's Daughter" echo anecdotes Mowatt relates in her autobiography. The book gives an invaluable backstage view of theater life in the early nineteenth century. Mowatt described the duties of the licensed puffer of the theater, the purpose of the assemblies of actors in the green-room, the role of the prompter, and the shabbiness of typical backstage quarters. Mowatt gave descriptions of the preparations her heroines take to play roles she herself enacted such as Desdemona, Virginia, and Evadne that give insight into what Mowatt's acting must have been like.

Although Mowatt's heroines endure much tragedy, *Mimic Life* is hilarious reading in spots such as the following describing my favorite Mowatt character, the disaster-prone Mrs. Pottle, in an incident happening in days when actors were required to supply their own costumes:

> Mrs. Pottle next strutted on the stage. Her stunted, shrivelled-up figure was almost concealed in the folds of her far-spreading train, fashioned in flame-colored cotton velvet. She had prodigally adorned her diminutive head with a huge crown, cut out of foil. It was of her own tasteful manufacture, and being somewhat limp in construction, shook and rattled at every movement. Such a peal of laughter as broke from the audience when she turned to them her wizened face! Mrs. Pottle had been occupying her leisure moments in the green-room in the laudable pursuit of plain sewing. She chanced, at the moment when Fisk made his call, to be more deeply engrossed by her housewifely avocation than her professional triumphs. The queen had pompously stalked upon the stage without removing the spectacles, which glittered just beneath her gilt-paper crown. The hand which she lifted to give point to her declamation showed one

finger armed with a shining brass thimble. The unconscious Pottle smiled benignly; and, when the diversion of the audience found vent in mocking applause, she curtseyed in the style in which she thought queens were wont to curtsey. It may be well to state that her conception of royalty was chiefly derived from the right regal dame chronicled in "Mother Goose" as diverting herself in the kitchen with the consumption of bread and honey.

Some individual in the gallery waggishly inquired whether her royal majesty had quite repaired the aperture in her royal consort's stocking. Mrs. Pottle's attention was consequently attracted to her thimble. She plucked the tell-tale armor, and hunted for a pocket; but pocket to her newly-made queenly garment there was none. She clutched at her spectacles; they were entangled in her hair, but, after, several furious pulls, gave way, dislodging the wonderful crown. It sent forth a tinsel sound, as it lightly dropped on stage. The merriment of the audience now reached its height. Mrs. Pottle was decidedly crestfallen.[26]

Mimic Life is, if nothing else, a marvelous document of nineteenth century American theater.

Twin Roses started as a story Mowatt intended to include in *Mimic Life*. She expanded it to novel length. It is the story of the misfortunes of the twin sisters Jessie and Jeanie Garnett. Both fall in love with actor Herman Landor. The book is much the same in tone and character as *Mimic Life*. Along with chronicling the twins' misadventures, Mowatt continued her fight to expose and nullify theatrical prejudice in passages like the following:

> In Virginia, a canon of the church prohibits its members from attending dramatic representations. Thus the acted drama seemed placed without the pale of good. [Jessie] knew nothing of the arguments which might be used in extenuation of so narrow an edict. Much that to her seemed the growth of bigotry did not deserve a name so solemnly harsh. Traditional prejudice—the excitement produced by the burning of a theater (1811), in which many valuable lives were lost—perhaps some abuses of the theater itself, and a want of desire, or power, to suppress them, on the part of the public—these causes might have furnished a fitter appellation for the source whence the edict emanated.[27]

In both *Twin Roses* and *Mimic Life*, Mowatt created sympathetic characters who suffer as a result of prejudice against the Theater.

In Mowatt's real life, things were not going well. Although biographer Marius Blesi vigorously denies problems in the Ritchie marriage, Anna Cora left her Richmond home in 1860 never to return. She originally traveled to be with her ailing father, who died on April 5, 1860. On August 25, 1860, she sailed for Europe without William Foushee to visit one of her sisters who was also ailing. In *Lady of Fashion*, biographer Eric Barnes speculated that there might have been a difference of opinion on the issues of slavery and states rights between the Ritchies and hinted that William Foushee might have had a black mistress.[28] Regardless of what the domestic situation was between the two, the outbreak of the Civil War effectively discouraged Anna Cora's potential return to Virginia. She lived in Paris from 1861-63. From there, she published *The Mute Singer, A Novel* in 1861.

The Mute Singer is the story of Sylvie de la Roche, again, like the characters of *Mimic Life*, a performer, but this time a singer rather than an actress. She is the daughter of extremely poor parents who do not recognize her talent, but is taken under the wing of their neighbor Maitre Beaujeau, a gruff old music teacher. He takes Sylvie on as a pupil and secures for her an opportunity to sing at the home of a rich count. She is a tremendous success, especially with young Marquis and Mademoiselle de St. Amar. Sylvie and the Marquis immediately fall in love, but she dares not hope to marry a man with such a high social position.

The count's concert master hires Sylvie, but the strains of rehearsals and excitement of performances cause her health to fail and she has a nervous breakdown. She recovers her health but seems to have permanently lost her voice. When her father is injured one day a few miserable weeks later, Sylvie, in a moment of panic, regains her singing, but not her speaking voice. Hence she becomes a mute singer. After much turmoil and melodramatic misunderstandings, Sylvie marries the Marquis and almost everyone lives happily ever after.

The Mute Singer was originally published in serial form in *The New York Ledger*. The story ran on the first page of the weekly issue of this publication from January 26, 1861, through March 30, 1861. It was evidently quite popular. Editor Robert Bonner bragged in an April 13, 1861, editorial that Empress Eugenie was among the novel's entranced readers:

> We learn, through a private letter from Paris, that on a recent occasion, while the maids of Eugenie were preparing her toilette prior to her going to a grand ball, she amused herself with reading Mrs. Ritchie's story of "The Mute Singer" in the Ledger. So absorbed did the Empress become in this fascinating story that she continued to read on after the maids had finished their work, without noticing that the hour had passed when she was to notify the Emperor of her readiness to depart. Napoleon, meanwhile, grew

impatient at the delay, and finally sent his chamberlain to notify the Empress that he was "awaiting her pleasure" whereby she was recalled to herself, and bade "The Mute Singer" goodbye until she should return.[29]

Whether or not the story actually found its way into the boudoir of the French Empress, it did enter many American homes. Robert Bonner claimed that in 1861 the *Ledger* made more money than any other American newspaper.

Anna Cora moved to Florence in 1863, where she produced *Fairy Fingers, A Novel* in 1865. In her article, "Anna Cora Ogden Mowatt Ritchie's Fairy Fingers: From Eugene Scribe's?," Patti Gillespie claimed that the plot and characters of Mowatt's 1865 novel are identical to Eugene Scribe's 1858 play *Les Doigts de fee*.[30] Both tell the same the story of a poor orphan of aristocratic stock, Madelaine, who falls in love with a count's son. After a series of misunderstandings, she flees to America and opens a dress shop that quickly becomes the talk of Washington society due to her great skill at sewing. The count and his family visit America on business. They encounter Madelaine again when she is hired to make a ball gown for the daughter of the family. Other complications ensue, but through various acts of selfless heroism, Madelaine wins the approval of the count and countess. The family is reconciled; the complications are resolved; and the young lovers marry.

Gillespie reasoned there are three possibilities that would account for the similarity between Scribe's play and Mowatt's novel: Mowatt drew from Scribe; Scribe drew from Mowatt; or both drew from a third source. Since Mowatt had a history of drawing inspiration from other sources, Scribe characteristically cited even minor contributors to his works, and Gillespie could find no third source for the plot, she concluded that it is probable that Mowatt took the plot of her novel from Scribe's play.[31] However, in a way that Scribe's text does not, Mowatt used the story of Madelaine the seamstress to comment on issues of health, the status of women, and the trials of working women. To Mowatt, on her own at this time and forced to be financially independent, these were all issues of crucial importance.

The Civil War deprived William Foushee of his fortune and primary means of income. Rather than returning to him in 1865, Anna Cora moved to England, hoping to resume her stage career. The damp climate brought on another attack of her chronic respiratory illness. She lived as an invalid, maintaining a meager income by selling articles on the London scene to American journals. Despite the longevity and severity of her illness, neither her husband nor any of her relatives were present when she died. Her old friend Epes Sargent was among the last people to visit her. He wrote:

> I saw her two days before her death, and never did I witness such perfect, cheerful tranquillity as she manifested. In that supreme moment, when death seemed to have his hand on her, her thoughts and conversation were all of others, not once of herself.[32]

Anna Cora Ogden Mowatt Ritchie died in Twickenham, England, on July 21, 1870. She was fifty-one years old. Her body was buried in Kensall Green Cemetery in London beside her first husband, James Mowatt.

CHAPTER 3

FASHIONING THE CHARM:
THE RHETORIC OF ANNA CORA MOWATT'S
AUTOBIOGRAPHY

> If there be anything more detestable than writing one's Autobiography, the individual who now essays the task would be glad to know what it is.[1]
>
> — William Pleater Davidge, actor

As Avrom Fleishman states in "Personal Myth: Three Victorian Autobiographers," when writing an autobiography, the author writes himself or herself, transposing self into verbal form. The process of writing is a process of discovering the writer's own nature and selecting appropriate terms in which to portray him or herself. Writing an autobiography is a process of "self-creation" or the formation of a recognizable individual out of metaphoric materials. In the case of autobiography, those metaphoric materials are specifically the language in which the remembered events of a life are set down.[2]

Additionally, an autobiographer must address the question of how the individual relates to what is outside the self. In his preface to *Approaches to Victorian Autobiography*, editor George P. Landow pointed out that what makes the Victorian autobiography a literary mode so representative of its time is a concern with this problematic relationship that lies close to the heart of all literature and all culture of that age. He characterized all the major literary figures of this era as engaged in "heroic attempts to strike a proper balance between the demands of society and self."[3]

As a woman and actress, Anna Cora Mowatt's social balancing act was doubly difficult. She had to negotiate what she perceived as her readership's negative impressions of both these social roles in order to position herself rhetorically as a sympathetic and authoritative narrative voice. Her autobiography reflects a constant process of negotiation sometimes even involving the simultaneous playing of conflicting roles.

As a measure of her success in combating her notions of public prejudice against her, *Autobiography of an Actress* (1853) was a best seller. Publishers Ticknor, Reed and Fields sold 20,000 copies of the book in the first six years it was in print. In 1859, 500 copies of a second edition sold. Mowatt, who received a royalty of fifteen cents on each $1.25 copy, made about $3700 off the venture. Five dollars a week was a reasonable working wage at this time.[4] With one exception, all the reviewers of the book remarked on its "charm." Nathaniel Hawthorne, who also worked for publishers Ticknor and Fields, wrote the publishers of the autobiography to say that he had chosen to send Mrs. Mowatt's book along with Thoreau's *Walden, A Week on the Concord, Merrimee Rivers,* and two other books to an English friend as samples of works which outstandingly exhibited both originality and distinctly "American characteristics."[5]

It is difficult to be certain exactly what connotations the word "charm" carried at the time these reviews were written. Broadly defined, to charm is to bewitch, to create irresistible attraction. In other words, "charm" is the act of creating an overwhelmingly positive impression.

In this chapter, I examine Mowatt's act of successfully creating a pleasing self for her public in her autobiography. Susan Lanser postulated in Fictions of Authority that the authority of a given voice or text is produced from a junction of social and rhetorical properties.[6] "Narration," as Lanser states, "entails social relationships and thus involves more than the technical imperatives for getting the story told."[7]

Anna Cora Mowatt used varied techniques in constructing a narrative stance that enabled her to appear genuine and unaffected. Mowatt was able to charm her public into acceptance of her life story by carefully fashioning not only a self, but a life story that would ultimately conform to her audience's desires.

When writing an autobiography, the Victorian writer immediately encountered a stylistic problem. Readers expect autobiographies to be written from a first person point of view. However, the "I" narrator carries several inherent difficulties. As David Goldknopf has pointed out, inevitably the writer/speaker is saying, "I am important enough for you to spend your time listening to me."[8] This was a difficult position for a Victorian woman. On what superior knowledge or experience could she base this claim to the reader's attention? The ideal "domestic angel" had no experience with the world outside her own household. Other than advice on domestic matters, it seemed that such a creature could have little to offer a reader.

Englishwoman Harriet Martineau's impressions of the general attitude towards women at this time painted a picture of the limited sphere of experience available for conventionally minded upper-class women of that era:

> I have seen the horror of a woman's having to
> work,—to exert the faculties which her Maker gave
> her;—the eagerness to ensure her unearned ease and
> rest; the deepest insult which can be offered to an
> intelligent and conscientious woman. I know the tone
> of conversation which is adopted towards women;

different in its topics and style from that which any man would dream of offering to any other man. I have heard the boast of the chivalrous consideration in which women are held throughout their woman's paradise; and seen something of the anguish of crushed pride, of the conflict of bitter feelings with which such boasts have been listened to by those whose aspirations teach them the hollowness of the system. The gentlemen are all unaware that women are not treated in the best possible manner among them.[9]

The first convention held for the purpose of discussing and advocating women's rights was held in 1848 in Seneca Falls, N.Y. In *Woman and Her Needs* (New York, 1851), Mrs. E. Oakes Smith, one of the early leaders in this movement, wrote of the backlash against women who did not conform to social expectations of passivity:

> The fear that a woman may deviate the slightest from conventionalism in any way, has become a nervous disease with the public. Indeed, so little is she trusted as a creation, that one would think she were made marvelously beautiful, and endowed with gifts of thought and emotion only for the purpose of endangering her safety—a sort of spiritual locomotive with no check-wheel, a rare piece of porcelain, to be handled gingerly—in fact, a creature with no conservative elements within herself, but left expressly thus, that men might supply them, and lead and guide, and coerce and cajole her, as it pleased him best. She is a blind angel, neither adapted to heaven nor earth in herself, but if submitting graciously to man's guidance, capable of filling a narrow, somewhat smoky, and uncertain nook on this small

planet, and possibly to win heaven through the perfection of suffering here.

Let her assert the laws of her being, let her say she is capable of more than this narrow sphere, that she grieves and frets in the cage, and the fault is grievous. She is ill-tempered, ambitious, unwomanly—as though womanhood had but one signification. It is even a reproach for her to have a will of her own. The voice of her own soul within her crying for space and recognition must be suppressed, lest she should be less subservient as a wife, and less humdrum as a mother.[10]

Despite this prejudice, many upper and middle class women were joining the workforce and engaging in the process of finding and expressing their own voice. Many women wrote. George Sand, George Elliot, Harriet Beecher Stowe, Emily Dickinson, and the Bronte sisters were all contemporaries of Anna Cora Mowatt. There were also hundreds of other women whose names and works did not create impressions as lasting on the American reading public. One of these, Mrs. M.O.W. Oliphant, wrote of the contemporary bias against Victorian "authoresses":

Women must put up with the inevitable grievance of being classed "female writers" just as Horace Walpole's "royal and noble authors" supports the classification which seems to point them out as fine amateurs superior to, and scarcely worthy of, the full honors of the literary profession.[11]

During this period, as Susan Lanser has pointed out, the "I" narrator, (at least in fiction) was considered by critics the only "proper" format for a woman writer to use.[12] One,

(Richard Holt Hutton) advanced the theory that "women's imaginative powers were so limited that they could not project themselves into the consciousness of their characters, especially male characters."[13]

Anna Cora Mowatt did not group herself with the emerging group of radical feminists. She seemed to disapprove of women like Martineau and Oakes. She once wrote of Harriet Martineau's comments on a different subject:

> If ever the "livery of Heaven" was stolen "to serve the devil in," it has been done by Miss Martineau, and her ally Mr. Atkinson, in their late atheistical work...[14]

Since she seemed to wish to stay within the boundaries of acceptable behavior for women of her class, Mowatt had to engage in what Patricia Spacks has identified as "the conflict between concealing and revealing, between self-denial and self-expression" as she, despite her assumption of the culturally valorized characteristic of womanly "selflessness," wrote a book about her self.[15]

Mowatt's book also carried the burden of being a theatrical autobiography, a form gaining in popularity but not literary respectability at this time. One writer has characterized such works as being "episodic, chatty, and, of course, self-aggrandizing," masquerades "moved from stage to page."[16] Theatrical autobiographies were nonetheless popular with book buyers. The popularity of such gossipy, self-oriented works may seem inconsistent with the controlled and self-effacing standards for public decorum demanded by the widespread cult of sensibility which governed modes of conduct particularly for the middle to upper-class Victorians who had the disposable income to make up a significant portion of the book-buying public. However, when one looks at the cult of sensibility, as

Thomas Postlewait did in his essay on Victorian theatrical autobiographies, as a cultural attempt to sanction private feelings as a measure of public ethos, then the problematic relation between inner and outer identity becomes a topic that would continue to concern many observers. The lives of actors, as well as acting techniques could therefore have served readers who wished to be perceived as "sincere" in their interpersonal interactions as guides for the complex task of creating and maintaining a believable public persona.[17]

Anna Cora Mowatt's identity as an actress formed an important part of the social context for her autobiography. The responses of her reviewers show that it also shaped her audience's response to the work. Mowatt's identity as a woman and an actress added conditions to the rhetorical contract that existed unspoken between her report of personal information and her readers' propensity to trust in the veracity of that information, between the degree of calculation involved in her self-revelation and readers' degree of willingness to serve as a sympathetic audience.

In her autobiography, Anna Cora Mowatt dealt with the problem of authority head-on from the very first sentence. "My autobiography," she stated boldly, "needs no preface. Its apology is a promise made to one who had the best right to demand such a pledge..."[18] Only in the very last paragraph of the book did she—in a manner typical of Victorian autobiographers—ask the reader's indulgence for "slips of the pen" such as the bad grammar and the "degree of egotism in the constant use of the first person singular."[19] The way Mowatt straightforwardly stated and restated her justifications for inflicting her life story on potential listeners throughout the book gives the text a highly rhetorical flavor. I summarize her arguments for narrative authority as follows:

1. She spoke from first-hand knowledge and personal experience.

2.   Her work was the fulfillment of a responsibility to fully inform those who might look on her as a role model.

3.   She had statements from men in positions of conventional respectability to corroborate her assertions.

I list these arguments in reverse of the order that Mowatt did in the autobiography.   Although Mowatt used her experience as an actress as a justification for the text implicitly throughout the autobiography, her most straightforward claim to authority on this basis comes at the beginning of the last chapter of her book under the chapter sub-heading of "My Claims to offer a Defense of the Stage." She stated:

I have been for eight years an actress. In the exercise of my vocation I have visited many theaters throughout this land and in Great Britain. This fact, perhaps, gives me some right to speak upon the stage as an institution; upon its uses and abuses; for I speak (in all humility be it said) from actual knowledge and personal experience. My testimony has, at least, the value of being disinterested; for I was not bred to the stage; I entered upon it from the bosom of private life; none who are linked to me by affinity of blood ever belonged to the profession; I am about to leave it of my own choice; and I bid it farewell in the midst of a career which, if it has reached its meridian, has not, as yet, taken the first downward inclination. I can have no object in defending the drama apart from the impulse to utter what I believe to be truth and an innate love and reverence for dramatic art.[20]

Mowatt's claim for the reader's attention by the virtue of

her experience is the most weakly stated of all her arguments for authority. "This fact, *perhaps*," she stated, "gives me authority to speak..." Mowatt emasculated her claim to authority with parenthetical phrases like "*in all humility be it said*" and "My testimony, *at least*, has the value of being disinterested.." (my italics). This appearance of modesty creates an appropriately sincere voice for a female narrator.

In the above quote, Mowatt took trouble to distance herself from the theatrical profession. She stated that she was not "bred to the stage" nor were any of her family ever actors. This denial of association is paradoxical when the reader considers that Mowatt is basing her claim to authority in this argument on her first-hand experience with the world of theater. This purposeful distancing is a sign, I think, of how deeply Mowatt judged that public prejudice ran against actors.

Thomas Postlewait has written that a performer's autobiography, "besides being a record of accomplishment, is an appeal like all performance for recognition, for approval, for love."[21] In constructing the self to be presented to the general public in an autobiography, the performer faces a dilemma, according to him, between the desire to be valued as a masked being and yet still to be loved despite this self-displacing and sometimes self-denying need for performance. This dilemma, I believe, is what caused Mowatt to hold back on her strongest claim on her status as an expert in the eyes of her audience.

Mowatt had no such reservations in presenting her second claim to authority. The following appears in the second paragraph of the text:

> If one struggling sister in the great human family,
> while listening to the history of my life, gain courage
> to meet and brave severest trials; if she learn to look
> upon them as blessings in disguise; if she be
> strengthened in the performances of "daily duties",

however "hardly paid"; if she be inspired with faith in the power imparted to a strong will, whose end is good, then I am amply rewarded for my labor.[22]

Casting herself in the role of mentor to naive young girls who might consider a career on the stage presented Mowatt at her most altruistic.   Under this responsible and benevolent guise, she exposed what she felt were unsupported popular conceptions of theatrical life and revealed the depth of her personal expertise, as in the following excerpt:

> Let me here venture to warn any enthusiastic young aspirant against adopting the stage, unless her qualifications—not to use a much abused word, and say her mission—seem particularly to fit her for such a vocation, unless she be strongly impelled by the possession of talents which are unquestionable, unless she be enamored of Art itself. But that the dangers of the profession are such as they are generally accredited to be, I do not believe; for I have known too many women bred upon the stage, whose lives were so blamelessly exemplary, whose manners were so refined, whose intellect so cultivated, that they would adorn any sphere of society. The subject is not one into which I can fully enter; but this let me say, that the woman who could be dazzled by the adulation bestowed upon her talents as an actress, would be dazzled and led astray in the blaze of a ball room, in the excitement of social intercourse, in any situation where those talents could be displayed, in any position where she could hear "the false glozings of a flattering tongue." And from these where will she be shielded except in utter seclusion?
>
> Unless the actress in anticipation is willing to

encounter disappointment in myriad unlooked-for shapes; to study incessantly, and find that her closest study is insufficient; to endure an amount and kind of fatigue which she never dreamed of before; if she feel "the grasshopper a burden," and the "crumpled rose leaf" an inconvenience to her slumber, I would bid her shun the stage. But if she be prepared to meet petty as well as formidable trials, (the former are often more difficult to bear than the latter), if she be sustained by some high purpose, some strong incentive; if she act in obedience to the dictates of the "stern lawgiver, Duty,"—then let her enter the profession boldly; by gracing, help to elevate the stage; and add hers to the purifying influences which may dwell within the walls of a theater as securely as in any other temple of art. Let her bear in mind that the sometimes degraded name of "actress" can be dignified in her own person. Let her feel, above all things, that the actress must excite reverence as well as admiration. The crowd must honor as well as worship. They can always be made to do the latter at the feet of genius; they can only be compelled to do the former when genius sheds its halo around higher attributes.[23]

At many junctures in her narrative, Mowatt addressed a fictive audience of stage-struck juvenile readers in a similar manner. The strategy allowed her to blunt the delivery of her criticism of people prejudiced against acting and actors. For example, in the above paragraph, her use of the phrase "the sometimes degraded name of 'actress'" alludes to such prejudice without making Mowatt sound overly accusatory or defensive.

Under the guise of motherly advice, Mowatt was even able to combat the reputation actresses had for sexual promiscuity when she offered her opinion on what she delicately referred to as a subject that "is not one into which I can fully enter." Her oblique reference to illicit sexuality is entirely within character for the role of mentor. As an advisor, she could discuss the sexual aspects of the theater world without risk of repulsing potential readers with what reviewers of other theatrical works negatively labeled "green room gossip" and "scandalmongering."

Taking an indirect approach to her subject matter by framing it as advice also allowed Mowatt to soften the self-aggrandizing aspect of her narrative as she displayed her first-hand knowledge of the theater. She concluded her description of her highly successful second year in the theatrical profession with the following solemn warning:

> If [an actress has] tasted of the tree of knowledge of the world, and been gifted with dearly-bought insight into realities, she knows that those who lavish these gifts and bestow these favors are oftener actuated by self-love than by love of her. They bow to the rising star because its effulgence is reflected back upon its votaries.[24]

A much different narrative voice would have been created if Mowatt had instead written, "Since I had tasted of the tree of knowledge of the world, and had been gifted with dearly-bought insight into realities, I knew that those who lavished these gifts and bestowed these favors were oftener actuated by self-love rather than by love of me." As mentor, Mowatt answered the implicit question that Goldknopf claims readers ask of first person narrators —"Why should we listen to you?" Adopting an indirect style additionally enabled her to create a sincere and humble narrative voice that could address a wide range of topics without offending her audiences' sense of propriety.

Another significant rhetorical strategy that Mowatt used was to borrow the authority of men. Before writing her autobiography, Mowatt already had something of an established reputation at the time as an author. She had written "Fashion," a wildly successful play, still being produced at the time of this book's writing. She had also published a few novels and several non-fiction articles in women's magazines under her own name and the pseudonym Helen Berkeley. Mowatt's letters to her publishers, Ticknor and Fields, make clear that she wrote this book under the full knowledge that it would be published. Despite the strong claims she could make for independence, Mowatt still relied heavily on the men as support for much of what she reported herself as saying, doing, or thinking in her autobiography.

In the first sentence of the book, Mowatt stated that she was writing in order to fulfill her promise to her late husband that she would at the end of her career as an actress author a book about her experiences. Mowatt referred to her husband many times throughout the book. Casting herself as the dutiful, sacrificing wife helped create an appropriately "selfless" persona to combat the self-aggrandizing tendencies inherent in writing an autobiography.

Sub-headings to the last chapter of the book, in which Mowatt presented an organized argument for the acceptability of the stage, read as follows:

My Claims to offer a Defence of the Stage.—Lord Bacon on the Drama.—Sir Joshua Reynolds.—D'Israeli.—The rude Attempts of Thespis.—Aeschulus.—Existence of Theaters at the Time of the first Christian Era.—The Apostles.—St. Paul's Quotations from three dramatic Poets.—The Parables and the Drama.—Dr. Isaac Watts.—The Emperor Marcus Aurelius upon the Stage.—Martin Luther.—The Rev. Dr. Knox.—Philip Melancthon.—Lord Bacon.—Dr. Blair.—Sir Philip Sidney.— Dr. Gregory.—Sir Walter Scott.—Calcraft.—Art.—Use and Abuse.—With whom it lies to reform the Errors of the Stage.—

Two Hundred clerical dramatic Authors.—Dramas of the Archbishop Gregory Nazianzen; of Apollinaris, Bishop of Laodicea.—Sir Thomas More.—Tragedies of Milton, of Dr. Edward Young, of Rev. H. Milman, Rev. Dr. Croly, Addison, Dr. Johnson, Coleridge, Thompson, Goldsmith, Miss Hannah More, Miss Joanna Baillie, Miss Mitford.—The Stage: Pope's Exposition and its Use; Crabbe's ditto; Shakespeare's.—My own Experience.—The true Position of Actors. —Their Rank in ancient Times.—The high social Position held by many Actors in the present Time. —A Word of Farewell to the Members of the Profession.—These Memoirs.[25]

This list provides a fairly clear outline of her argument. Except for Misses More, Baille, and Mitford, all the authorities Mowatt drew on are male. Of them she stated:

> This is high authority in favor of the drama. As a strong aid to my own imperfectly expressed arguments in its defence, I cull a few opinions from sources which command reverence, out of the multitude that might be given, did space allow. The authorities I shall cite are such as should make any man pause before he ventures unconditionally to denounce the stage.[26]

Mowatt borrowed the undisputed authority of men in other more subtle ways. For instance, she explained her early aversion to the drama:

> For some years our parents and their children had all attended the church of Dr. E——n, now Bishop E——n. I loved to see him enter the Sunday School; I loved to see him in the pulpit; and was happier all day if he accidentally bestowed upon me a passing word. He disapproved of theaters; he pronounced them the

"abodes of sin and wickedness." It never occurred to
me to inquire what he really knew of theater; but I
trusted implicitly in his supposed information.[27]

Dr. Manton Eastburn, to whom Mowatt refers as Dr. E—n,
was a powerful source of authorization for anti-theatrical bias.
In the above paragraph she presented the minister as a person
young Anna looked up to and also as someone who had enough
support and respect in his community and profession to become
a bishop in later years. A devoutly religious person, Mowatt
habitually assumed in this and several other incidents in the
book that her readers shared her profound respect for religion
and religious figures. Without denigrating Eastburn as a person
or a professional, Mowatt undermined his position as an
individual qualified to speak on the relative merits of the
theater. "It never occurred to me," she says, "to inquire what
he *really* knew of theater..." (her italics). Mowatt chose not to
confront Eastburn directly but her clear implication is that the
minister had never been in a theater and therefore could not
know what he was talking about.

Instead of refuting Eastburn with her own experience,
Mowatt placed another male authority in contrast with
Eastburn's views. Mowatt's father, Charles Ogden, whose
formidable lineage and reputation she spent a large part of the
first chapter establishing, was a patron of the theater. Ogden
had the first-hand experience with the drama that Eastburn
lacked. Mowatt attended a play for the very first time at her
father's urging. She described the experience as follows:

When we first entered the boxes, my first
sensation was of bewilderment at the crowds, the
lights, the music, the sea of expectant faces beneath us
in the pit, and mounting waves around us and above
us. Yet I did not quite forget that there must be some

"sin and wickedness" which I could not comprehend, and I believe I even asked my father to have the goodness to point out the "harm." He might have told me, what I learned in later years, that the "harm" consisted in the perversion of good to evil; in abuses which had nothing to do with the drama itself; in the poison which evil minds, like spiders, draw from the rose whence the bee sucks but honey.[28]

Although Mowatt was converted from her anti-theatrical preconceptions by her first-hand experience, she rhetorically positioned her refutation of Eastburn's charges against the theater as coming from her father's mouth. She did not positively say that the opinions even came directly from her father but tempered her claim by stating that she believed that she asked her father to have the goodness to point out the "harm" in attending plays. He might have told her what she parenthetically tells us that she learned in later years about anti-theatrical prejudice. The opinion is Mowatt's, but she presented it as proceeding not merely from her own experience, but from the tutelage of her father, a male figure of unimpeachable authority by Mowatt's standards.

Thus in this anecdote, as in several other instances throughout the book, Mowatt converted her holding of controversial views or taking questionable actions into part of her responsibility as a dutiful wife, an obedient daughter, or a diligent student of the "great minds" of Western literature and culture. By putting others first and herself last in claiming authority to speak, Mowatt was able to keep the illusion of selflessness consistent with the idealized vision of a woman of sensibility while writing a book that was essentially a definition and celebration of her self.

Once Mowatt found a voice to tell her story that she felt her public could accept and find attractive, she was still faced with the problem of the tale itself. In the article "Biblical

Typology and the Self-Portrait of the Poet in Robert Browning," Linda H. Peterson pointed out that structuring, the shaping of the events of the autobiographer's life as a whole into a coherent pattern or relating of a limited number of events to a pattern, is the autobiographer's central task. The pattern for these life events is not necessarily inherent in the events themselves, but is discovered in or imposed upon those events by the autobiographer. The writer must create order out of the chaotic events of his/her life without falsifying the facts of his/her experience. In this process of discovering or creating an appropriate structure, the autobiographer may borrow structures from previous autobiography, from fiction, history, poetry, and other forms of discourse, altering them to suit the particular needs of the task he/she faces.[29]

In *Writing a Woman's Life,* Carol Heilbrun argues that women biographers and autobiographers have no established "script" for their life stories to fall into that their audience can immediately recognize and comfortably accept as natural and even predict the outcome. She said that men's life stories are often fitted to the familiar "quest" pattern from mythology. Personal failures, confusion, indecision, are all merely obstacles to be inevitably overcome in the fulfillment of the hero's destiny.[30] In a time when it would not seem appropriate, acceptable, or even natural for a woman to be in charge of her life, the quest pattern had to be modified. A woman's destiny ultimately lay in finding the appropriate man, or in the case of women like Florence Nightingale, the appropriate *men* to serve.

It might be more accurate to say that rather than having no script for life stories, women were excluded from using certain patterns demarcated as male. Clearly, the modified quest in which the woman finds her self-sacrificing vocation is a pattern and a very familiar one too. Heilbrun described this pattern as the "romance" script. Conversely, there is also the familiar "fallen woman" script, evoked memorably by Tolstoy's fictional *Anna Karenina,* in which a woman "falls," usually sexually, from society's expectations, suffers, then ultimately repents. Generalizing broadly, I would say that this view gives a woman two basic choices for framing her life experiences: either she can reify the path she took—see it as a progression towards a final justification; or she can express regret for those choices —see them as ultimately leading to error that can be atoned only by offering a cautionary confession. Another viable possibility for a writer would be creating a picaresque framework for her narrative. Episodes are unrelated. No overarching mission or meaning unifies the narrative. There are examples of women autobiographers and biographers of women choosing this route, but the price is that, in our positivistic way of perceiving the world, a story without a point is pointless, a mere amusement. Heilbrun complained that such stories cannot serve as myth/models for generations of women to come because they celebrate their uniqueness of circumstance. They create no comfortable path to follow.

To some extent, Mowatt's story must fall into this last category. Hers cannot properly be classified as a quest story. She does not really seem to be led to any inevitable fate by her adventures. She is also definitely not a classic fallen women. She almost fits the pattern that Carol Heilbrun calls a "moratorium," in which the persona must break with society to discover his/her true path. "The condition" Heilbrun says, "is marked by a profound sense of vocation, with no idea what that vocation is, and by a strong sense of inadequacy and deprivation."[31] What is missing from Mowatt's story is the inadequacy and deprivation. She was quite happy as a private, young married woman. Also missing is any display of deep satisfaction with the vocation she seemed ultimately destined for—writing for and acting in the theater. Because Mowatt perceived her society as strongly disapproving of the theater, she could not relish it openly.

To get around these structural difficulties, Mowatt, who was at the time of writing already a successful novelist and playwright, turned to techniques that were quite literary. Although a critical reader could discover a variety of tactics Mowatt used to render her life story readable, I wish to concentrate on the two structuring techniques I feel comprise the primary thrust of her rhetorical strategy: 1) the use of anecdotes as *mise en abyme* and 2) the echoing story patterns from popular fiction.

Theatrical biographies and autobiographies are typically full of anecdotes. Part of the function and charm of such writing projects is the revelation of small personal stories about the subject and life in theater. Mowatt's book is no exception. However, rather than allowing them to function only as brief, unrelated glimpses into her private and professional life, Mowatt used several of these small stories within the larger narrative to underline her overall argument. In this way they serve as what narratologists call *mise en abyme*.

The term *mise en abyme* originally comes from heraldry. A figure in an escutcheon is said to be *en abyme* when it constitutes a miniature of that escutcheon. In his *Dictionary of Narratology*, Gerald Prince defines *mise en abyme* as "a miniature replica of a text embedded within that text."[32] These embedded narratives are textual segments that reduplicate, reflect, or mirror one or more aspects of the textual whole.

Mowatt gave us several miniature portraits of women in the theater who fit the outline of the character she was attempting to sketch of herself in her autobiography. Take for example, her description of the Misses Wheatley, whom she saw dance the same night she decided to go to theater for the first time to see Fanny Kemble:

> I little thought that in after years I should have the pleasure of becoming acquainted with them; no longer children but the most refined and accomplished ladies, exemplary wives,—one of them a mother,— and both gracing the high sphere in which they move.

> Their stage garments have long been laid aside; but
> the stage needs no better defense than the blameless
> lives of these two admirable and lovely women and
> their mother.[33]

Almost ignoring their professional accomplishments, Mowatt praised the two ladies for their social and familial achievements. As Mowatt herself was preparing to do, the performers had "laid aside the garments of the stage." The Misses Wheatley had emerged from their exposure to the theater untainted by any supposed wickedness of the profession.

As if to make certain that her readers would note her argument, Mowatt at one point related three stories in a row of what she called the "sorely tried servants of the stage." She explained that she was doing so in "illustration of the mental discipline practised by actors, and of their absolute self-renunciation, in laying aside the most heartrending sorrows during the fulfillment of their duty."[34] All three actors were women. All three, like the image Mowatt strove to project of herself, demonstrate admirable devotion to conventional values despite their unconventional profession. The first was Mrs. Parker, an actress who had to deal, as Mowatt did, with the long illness and death of her husband.

> Mrs. Parker, a most estimable woman and
> excellent actress, was the representative of Prudence
> in London. While the play was in rehearsal she
> suddenly received a telegraphic dispatch from
> Brighton, announcing that her husband was at the
> point of death. She hastened to him, and arrived in
> time to receive his dying thanks and parting words of
> tenderness. They had been united for twenty-five
> years. The bond of mutual love between them seems
> to have been the most holy kind, proved by love's

highest tests—constancy and unselfishness. For years the devoted wife had supported her invalid husband and their children by her exertions on the stage.[35]

As she lavished understanding praise on Mrs. Parker, Mowatt was teaching her readers how she wished them to interpret the story of her own relationship to James Mowatt and decision to embark on her dramatic career. Mrs. Parker, Mowatt insisted, was motivated to her success on the stage not out of a desire for self-aggrandizement, but out of financial necessity and devotion to her invalid spouse.

Mrs. Knight, Mowatt's next suffering servant of the stage, was similarly selfless:

Mrs. Knight was the original personator of Prudence in New York. Her name is endeared to the American public by a host of pleasant associations. Her talents were long the delight of audiences who used to crowd the Park Theater in the good old times. When I became acquainted with her she was a widow, residing with her brother, with whom she had a sort of twin-like attachment. Her hopes were all centered upon an only daughter, a lovely being of seventeen. When Mrs. Knight was first presented to me this sweet girl stood by her side, eagerly listening to our conversation. I can vividly recall the delicate bloom of her cheek, the lustrous eyes, the finely-rounded form, that seemed glowing with health and the enjoyment "of life's pure pleasures manifold." We never met again until *Fashion* was reproduced after my own debut, and I enacted the character of Gertrude. Mrs. Knight personated Prudence, as before. Grief had made such ravages in her face that I scarcely recognized her when we encountered each other behind the scenes. Her daughter's summons had come, shortly after I first saw her, in the form of consumption. She lingered a few months, filling her mother's breaking heart with alternate hopes and fears, and then departed. The bereaved mother had been completely crushed by the blow; yet there she stood, fantastically attired for a comedy, though life had become to her the saddest of tragedies. I watched her when she appeared on the stage, and could not perceive that her performance had lost any of the humor by which it had been formerly characterized; but in reality, every look, every word, every action was a mere mechanical effort—the body went through a set routine while the spirit was far away. When she left the stage, I twice saw her throw herself into a chair and burst into a flood of tears. At the stage summons, the scalding drops were hastily wiped away; but they seemed to reflow spontaneously the instant she was no longer within sight of the audience.[36]

In a significant parallel that Mowatt did not point out, both of Mowatt's adopted children died of consumption. She led us to believe that in Knight's case (and allowed the reader to extrapolate about Mowatt's own life) the loss of her daughter negated any emotional satisfaction or sensual pleasure that could be derived from performance or public adulation.

This alienation from the sensual led to the sort of stoicism exhibited by the anonymous heroine of the last anecdote of the trio:

Mr. Macready was representing Macbeth at Drury Lane. An actress of great public and private excellence personated Lady Macbeth. She was in the act of going upon the stage, when a letter was placed in her hands by the messenger of the theater. She glanced at the handwriting and turned deadly pale—but her cue had been spoken by Macbeth. She thrust the letter in her bosom, and walked firmly upon the stage. When the curtain fell upon the close of the third act, my friend saw her with trembling hands hastily tear open the missive. She uttered one exclamation of intense agony, and with a face rigid as marble, but tearless eyes, refolded the epistle. My friend asked her what had happened; but she could not command herself to answer. Stifling down her emotion, she hurried to her dressing room. The curtain rose on the fourth act. At the call boy's summons she reappeared, and with forced composure concluded the part of Lady Macbeth. It was not until the curtain fell, and her professional duty was at an end for the night, that her grief broke forth in tears and words. The letter apprised her of the death of her husband, whom she had watched over with the truest womanly devotion through the most terrible of trials. He was a lunatic.[37]

Read in the context of the argument Mowatt was making about her own life in the theater, the above story is more than just another illustration of the well-worn theatrical mandate "the show must go on." As Mowatt seemed to indicate by saving her dramatic announcement of the nature of husband's illness for the last line, the actress's confrontation with the death of her spouse while in the midst of performing a major role was merely culmination of a much longer period of publicly suppressed suffering. Mowatt presented these three actresses not as the tough, independent, career-minded women a reader might reasonably see them to be, but as vulnerable, self-sacrificing ladies, dependent on their husbands and family for emotional satisfaction. In her effusively sentimental and supportive descriptions of what she framed as the tragic self-sacrifice of these women, Mowatt tutored the reader in what she considered the ideal reception of similar incidents in her own life story.

Narratologist Marie MacLean has called the *mise en abyme* an "eminently theatrical" literary device, comparing it to the *tableau vivant* so popular in Victorian drama. Both stress the iconic value of the portrayal of selected moments in a narrative. The framed spectacle serves the obvious purposes of enhancement and illustration. However each "frozen moment" also acts as a microcosm to the macrocosm of the text. "On this internalized stage," MacLean states, "we see *en abyme* not just the actors within the frame, but the spectator as voyeur."[38]

Mowatt modestly, yet highly rhetorically, cast other actresses in the role of her self when she sympathetically interpreted her career decision. She cast herself in the role of the ideal spectator in what I term her "conversion" story. In her description of her decision to go see Fanny Kemble in a play, Mowatt created a miniature representation of her fictive audience. Mowatt, significantly here presented as an intelligent, open-hearted, but inexperienced child, learned anti-theatrical notions from a respected clergyman—as many of her readers with similar prejudices had done. Mowatt stated that she conceived her desire to go see the famous actress not from any idiosyncratic private longings but from knowledge of Kemble's public reputation, as she reported in the following:

> (Fanny Kemble's) name was on everybody's lips; her praises echoed on all sides. I read critiques upon her acting in all the papers and heard her talked of as a most devoted daughter and truly excellent woman. I could not help longing to see her; but the old objections were strong within me, and I was afraid of being laughed at if I confessed that my interest in the

woman made me willing to enter such a place, as I supposed the theater to be, to see the actress.[39]

Mowatt painted herself as an individual drawn to the theater not out of prurient curiosity or for purposes of sexual gratification, but out of admiration for intellectual/professional accomplishments and social/moral respectability of an individual actress. Mowatt wished us to read her life in just the same way, with a willingness to abandon formerly held prejudices and to respect what she, now acting the same role of the experienced mentor that her father performed, told us was respectable. In this way, Mowatt interpolated the reader into a position of conversion. The narrative as a whole therefore becomes the reader's conversion story, in which the spectator in a manner parallel to Mowatt's experience with Fanny Kemble, is led to an intellectual/professional/moral respect for actresses and the theater itself through an encounter with a respectable actress.

Since Anna Cora Mowatt was a prolific writer of popular melodramas, it would not be a surprising choice for her to arrange and present her life story in a form and plot structure that corresponded to melodrama. However the correspondence is not complete even though autobiography does share several characteristics of melodrama. For example, Balukhatyi listed impassioned speech and vivid emotional relationships between the characters as two elements in his itemization of characteristics of melodrama.[40] Both of these exist in abundance in Mowatt's book, as in the following excerpt, where Anna Cora confided her intention to begin a career as an actress to her sister:

> It was the most trying duty to make my intended debut known to my family. My sister May was, of course, the first in whom I confided. She was of a

gentle and timid nature, and shrank in alarm from the proposed public step. She could not discuss it without tears and violent emotion.

"You cannot go through with it—I am sure you cannot!" were her weeping exclamations.

"We none know what we can do until we are tried," was the truism with which I answered her objection.

"What will our friends say of you if you make a public appearance?" she urged.

"What will our friends do for us in case I do not? Will they preserve to us this sweet home? Will they support us? Will they even sympathize with our adversity?"

"But you will lose your position in society."

"If I fail, probably I shall; but I do not intend to fail. And what is that position in society worth when we are no longer able to feast and entertain? How many of those whom we feasted and entertained at our last ball will seek us out when we live in poverty and obscurity?"

"If you would only look at all the obstacles!"

"No, I am looking above and beyond them, and I see only duty in their place."[[41]

This emotional scene between the two sisters demonstrating May's passionate concern and giving Anna Cora the opportunity to defend her plans in a speech that could have easily played on stage as a dramatic soliloquy also qualifies as an example of what Balukhatyi calls "strikingly effective situations" or situations susceptible to obvious "sentimental" treatment. Mowatt did not coolly and methodically present her position on the acceptability of the theater here as she later did in the last chapter of her book. Instead of rational argument, at this high point of interest in her life story where she openly broke with conventional expectations of a woman of her social class, Mowatt gave the reader an affecting scene between her weeping, caring sister and her brave, noble self.

The similarities between Mowatt's autobiography and popular melodrama begin to break down, however, when one looks at the overall plot structure. Balukhatyi outlines the typical melodramatic scenario as follows:

Public event involves protagonist,

1) Protagonist becomes suspect,
2) Love,
3) Villainy disclosed,
4) Protagonist endangered,
5) Spectacle/Public climax,
6) Protagonist exonerated.[42]

One could say that the autobiography conforms to this pattern to the extent that Mowatt, the protagonist, becomes involved with the public debate over the acceptability of the theater, her reputation is endangered by prejudiced peers, then she is exonerated by her ability to remain a moral person while having a successful stage career. Like a character from one of the stories by her popular contemporary Charles Dickens, Mowatt can be read as an innocent who makes her way through the trials of an unfair and oppressive society revealing its abuses. The suspense of her story comes from the constant danger that some of life's adversities will make her lose her bourgeois morality. Like Dickens' *Nicholas Nickleby* or *Oliver Twist*, Mowatt fell in with the roughest of company, but emerged unscathed and triumphantly middle class. However, such comparisons conform more to the form than the spirit of melodrama. One could not characterize the plot of Mowatt's autobiography as Balukhatyi does the typical melodrama as involving "extreme violations of the normal connections among everyday phenomena." Mowatt's life story as she presented it does not have the violent sensationalism that so typifies melodrama.

Part of the reason the autobiography fails to conform to the typical characteristics of melodrama lies in Mowatt's unsuitability as a melodramatic protagonist. Women in melodramas were usually portrayed as "angels." As David Grimstead states in *Melodrama Unveiled*, writers often affixed concepts such as salvation and redemption to the heroine's role. Melodrama's "angel women" were guardian angels whose functions were to guide, protect, and solace erring man.[43] By emphasizing her selfless devotion to male figures such as her husband and her father, Mowatt painted herself into the role of "angel woman." However, as Grimstead emphasizes, the heroine as angel cannot fill the center of a melodrama, which requires conflict of some sort.[44] "Angel women" excelled in passive qualities like modesty, patience, and meekness—all characteristics inappropriate to the role of protagonist. Tension and excitement in melodrama grows from the fragility of both the heroine's position and the concept of virtue she represents. Thus the early parts of Mowatt's life story where she portrayed herself as an intelligent, independent, yet vulnerable young girl read most like melodrama. However, the more she settled her self-portrayal into the role of a devoted matron and wise, dutiful adult role model, the more dramatic tension goes out of her life story.

Another way the autobiography fails as melodrama is in its weak identification of the villains of the piece. As Grimstead states, the melodramatic villain took two basic shapes, one for comedy and one for serious plays. The comic villain, though wholly despicable and unprincipled, remained too obviously foppish and ridiculous to pose a real threat. The serious villain showed enough intelligence or courage to become a frightening devil incarnate.[45] Mowatt fit none of the antagonists in her life story into either mold. Although in a few cases, she mentioned individuals like Dr. Eastburn (though never identified them by their full name) who held views that contradicted Mowatt's own or took actions she disapproved of, she usually identified those that opposed her in a generalized way as in the following excerpt:

> I pondered long and seriously upon the consequences of my entering the profession. The *"qu'en dira t'on?"* of Society had no longer the power to awe me. Was it right? was it wrong? were questions of higher moment. My respect for the opinions of "Mrs. Grundy" had slowly melted away since I discovered that, with that respectable representative of the world in general, success sanctified all things; nothing was reprehensible but failure.[46]

Other than disapproving social peers, whom Mowatt identified under the blanketing term "Mrs. Grundy" (a fictive name commonly used at this time to refer collectively to the socially conservative elements of polite society), the main source of opposition to Mowatt's chosen profession came from individuals within organized religion. She typically referred to these individuals as follows:

> Let not the so called religious world start at this assertion; we know what we say, and we fearlessly assert that there is many a poor, despised player, whose Christian graces of faith, patience, charity, and self-denial put to shame the vaunted virtues of the proud pharisee; nor are they always the purest who talk most about purity.[47]

The antagonists of Mowatt's life story were not only her peers, but a significant portion of her fictive audience. The rhetorical thrust of the text is to convince people prone to discount or disrespect her because of her connections to the theatrical world of her own respectability and the respectability of theater. Since Mowatt's antagonists were potentially the very people she was addressing, she could not paint their characters so black as to alienate them. Without running the risk of offending, she could not portray those who opposed her as the fools or villains required to give her life story true melodramatic tension. The purpose of Victorian melodrama was to sensationalize experience, violently provoking emotions of fear and pity. Although Mowatt's rhetoric also played on the emotions on her reader, her overall approach to her audience was different. She made a concerted appeal to both their emotions and their intellect. Elements of melodrama gave her life story pathos designed to underline and emphasize her logical appeals. Mowatt required from her readers both a clear head and a sympathetic heart.

Although Mowatt's autobiography was generally well-received critically, at least one of the reviewers did not buy her justifications. The reviewer from the *London Athenaeum* believed that the book's only readers were "persons curious about curious literature." The book, according to this reviewer, had a place only in the library of books by the "ill-advised" where books of female autobiographers are particularly prominent. Autobiographies by former actresses in particular make "curious contributions." The critic complained of too many "deliberate compliments to 'my genius, my sweetness, my beauty, my simplicity and my ingenuity.'"[48]

Mowatt knew that she had no defense against auditors that were fundamentally opposed to works by women in general and actresses in particular. After all, her potential reader had to be able to get past the title *Autobiography of an Actress*. But for those willing to suspend judgment at least temporarily and give her a hearing, Mowatt took steps to paint a picture other than the egotistical writer extolling "my beauty, my sweetness" seen by the *Atheneaum*. For example, in her letters to her publishers prior to the publishing of the autobiography, Mowatt's most persistent concern seems to be with a picture of her that was printed as the book's frontispiece. She insisted, "Send me an impression of the engraving; that is an *important* part of the work" (her italics).[49] The picture that was printed is of her in profile, smiling slightly. The portrait seems to capture in a nutshell the qualities that Mowatt wished her readers to find in her.

Mowatt's rhetorical strategies did seem to work for many of her readers. The majority of her reviewers seemed to recognize that her act of being charming in this book was a purposeful and successful one. One reviewer opened his review with "Mrs. Mowatt is an actress who is her own Barnum."[50] The reviewer for the *Home Journal* said, "the great charm of the book is its naïveté and evident candor."[51] *Harper's* claimed, "the apparent simplicity and genuine unction with which she narrates her adventures give to her volume something more than even the natural charm of autobiography."[52] The reviewer for *Putnam's* praised it saying:

> Mrs. Mowatt's autobiography ... is precisely such a volume as its title does not promise, for we naturally anticipate a piquant, egotistical, frivolous, and green-roomish narrative full of rouge, spangles, and false sentiment, but instead, we have a simply-told story of an earnest and heroic woman, whose life has been one of contention with adverse fortune, sweetened by many brilliant successes, which were the result of her own exertions.[53]

Alexander Woollcott, remembering the book in the *New York Times*, January 28, 1917, stated that the narrative "recalls that most charming heroine in English fiction—Elisabeth Bennett."[54]

Mowatt was able to get around the difficulties of writing as a woman in the first person by giving solid, believable, acceptable reasons for writing and creating a writing persona that appeared frank, candid, and genuinely humble. Mowatt was able to fashion a self that was not proud, not self-aggrandizing, and not threateningly aggressive. Anna Cora Mowatt's autobiography charmed her public because she was able to establish convincingly her authority by skillfully employing rhetorical strategies that compensated for the biases she anticipated her story would encounter. She created a narrative voice that readers could feel comfortable indulging with their attention. Mowatt also provided a narrative framework for her life story that was familiar, attractive and pleasing to her auditors. In the absence of an appropriate pattern for women's life stories, she borrowed from popular fiction to create both a teller and a tale that worked the magical spell that transformed the autobiography of an actress to a delightful story of woman of simple charm.

CHAPTER 4

SEDUCTIONS OF THE HALF-SEEN WORLD:
THE DEFENSE OF THE CREATED SELF IN
ANNA CORA MOWATT'S FICTION

Anna Cora Mowatt wrote several popular novels. Out of the selections of her fiction available, I chose *Mimic Life* for examination in this chapter because I was intrigued by the fact that Mowatt insisted on calling this fictive work autobiographical. Mowatt published this collection of short stories about the theater two years after her *Autobiography of an Actress*. Why did she do so? What more about her life needed to be said after she had told all in the autobiography? My answer to these questions is that I believe Mowatt wished to use the authoritative public voice that she had so carefully created to carry on her fight against the anti-theatrical bias she found in her peers. The pervasively negative stereotypes Victorians held of actors, actresses, and the theater in general made the image Mowatt strove to create in her autobiography of herself as a lady and an actress an oxymoron. The bad reputation of actresses in general had threatened Mowatt's own carefully constructed reputation. This lack of respect for the Theater and its workers made it more difficult for Mowatt to establish narrative authority in her autobiography. Paradoxically, she chose to continue her fight to salvage the Theater's reputation and therefore her own through narrative.

As an actress, Mowatt found herself in a profession widely considered to be not only unacceptable for a lady, but also immoral. Through textual strategies employed in *Mimic Life*,

Mowatt strikes the balance between conforming to conventional expectations and defying or attempting to change them. Through the creation of sympathetic characters and narratives filled with pathos, she attempted to turn the tide of contempt which she believed many conventional Victorians held for theater and its workers.

Theater's bad reputation with conventional Victorians stemmed largely from its associations with sex and sexual display. The period of Western History we Westerners call the Victorian age began with a sexual revolution. Before the eighteenth century, sex in Western Culture was a bodily function that could be publicly discussed—even in "decent" society. During the Victorian age, however, sexuality was transformed into a subject that was only properly discussed privately between members of a legally sanctioned, procreative couple.[1]

In my opinion, because theater, bound to earlier traditions, still made sex a thing for display outside of the jurisdiction of the family, theater became a target for disapprobation. The rhetorical position implicitly argued by allowing sex to be presented in a public forum made the theater a site of discomfort and tension for the Victorian mind. The proper Victorian was against it, but because sex had become the unspeakable, s/he could not explicitly state why. Because of their deeply held belief that sex should be private and familial, the theater was improper. However, because the same belief made sex a topic that was publicly unspeakable, the proper Victorian denied him/herself the subtleties of language to explain sufficiently its impropriety.

I feel Victorian pornography was a point of cultural "slippage" where free and explicit discussion of the impropriety of sex as made manifest on the public stage occurred. Not only the "decent" Victorians saw theater as a site of shame and scandal. Creators and consumers of erotic material relished that indecency. The treatment of the world of the theater in

Victorian pornography made the linkage between sex and the theater explicit.

Despite the fact that this sexual stigma originated on the level of folkloric fiction supported only by rumor and the occasional sensational scandal covered by the tabloid press, the taint of impropriety cast on the Victorian theater by pornographers was real to its audience. The anti-theatrical prejudice spawned by the linking of perverse sexuality and theater in certain media of the popular culture affected even those who had no first hand knowledge of the stereotypes of pornography. Real actresses had to strive to fit comfortably into society with this sort of condemnation of them in the "common knowledge" as backdrop and baggage. To make matters worse for the advocates of theater, pornography, like acceptable sex, was private. Although pornography fit the Victorian ideal for the discussion of sex through its privacy, when its practitioners went public with their activities, Victorian society censored and punished them like all other nonproductive and not family-oriented expressions of sexuality. Therefore advocates of the theater could not refute the testimony of Victorian erotica with frank openness because society did not acknowledge the existence of such material.

In contrast with the view of the theater as sensual and debased was the more cerebral and spiritual picture of theater life as painted by Anna Cora Mowatt in her book *Mimic Life*, a collection of short stories about life in the theater. Although she probably had no direct knowledge of Victorian pornography about the theater, it is my belief that her stories are a rebuttal to the pervasive public image that pornography revealed.

There were very real intersections between the theater world and the demi-monde. John Elsom calculates that the uneasy relationship between the Western stage and prostitution dates back to the time when young male actors impersonating women on the public stage were replaced by real females.[2] I would say the relationship goes back much further. In Ancient Rome, women performers were frequently said to double as prostitutes. The first permanent theaters in London, built in the time of Shakespeare, were next door neighbors to brothels. The semi-secluded stalls of theaters frequently were used for purposes other than viewing plays. Although in the nineteenth century reformers like Macready (circa 1830) took great pains to drive away the prostitutes and establish strict codes of moral behavior for actors, near the end of the century George Bernard Shaw could still make the following damning accusation of an anonymous London playhouse:

> The theater is not really a theater. It is a drink shop and a prostitution market: and the last shred of its disguise is stripped by the virtually indiscriminate issue of free tickets to men. Access to the stage is easily obtained: and the plays preferred by the management are those in which the stage is filled by young women who are not in any serious technical sense of the word actresses at all... it is an intolerable evil that respectable managers should have to fight against the free tickets and disorderly housekeeping of unscrupulous competitors.[3]

A prostitute picked up by the police, he claimed, was likely to give her profession as "actress."[4]

Seeking to make the theater more respectable, Queen Anne passed a law forbidding members of the public to go backstage during the course of performances. Popular belief held that orgies took place in the theaters' green rooms.[5] Such restrictions made the theater's character even more suspicious by curtaining off its mundane workings from public view. Restricting access made the theater even more a site for speculation and fantasy. Other things associatively linked actresses and prostitutes. Like prostitutes, actresses were professional "women of the night." They made their living by successfully suing for men's attention. Each made herself recognizably eligible for the male gaze. Like prostitutes, actresses routinely violated conventions of dress, make-up, gesture, and association that distinguished "respectable" women from the demi-monde.[6] Thus, just as the public assumed that theaters that did not make extraordinary efforts to combat the image of the covert brothel were soaked in sexual impropriety, so they assumed an actress was a prostitute until she gave proof to the contrary.

Undoubtedly, the gulf between the conventions of theatrical costume and "normal" standards of dress contributed to the public's perception of theater as improper. Sexuality for the Victorians was restricted and private. The voluminous and concealing clothing they wore was an outward symbol of their attitude toward the proper privacy of sex. In a way more blatant than any prostitute would have dared, theatrical costume violated the dress codes of the street and the drawing room. Ankles, calves, legs, thighs, crotch, and upper torso were both revealed and flaunted.

Theatrical costume of the period fetishized the female form. Costume went beyond the requirements of dramatic reality to reveal the feminine form as such. These constant and very public reminders of the gender of adult female performers served as indicators of not only sex but also the sexuality of those women for the privacy-minded Victorians. This was a freedom that was out of reach for even the most daring of the non-theatrical public. Research in the Private Case and non-restricted materials of the British Library and the collections of the Kinsey Institute for Research in Sex, Gender, and Reproduction reveal that the theater in general, and actresses in particular, appear so frequently in Victorian erotica that acting was the most often particularized occupational type of women.[7] As "cheerleader" or "stewardess" can have risqué connotations today, so did the words "actress" or "theater" in those days. Unlike the other stock characters, real actresses were implicated by their fictionalizations in pornography. There were plenty of lewd maids in dirty books, but it was highly unlikely that you would find a maid you knew mentioned by name. This was not the case for actresses as this summary of William Jeffs' *Le Chassepot* attests,

> Mlle. Leonie Leblanc, the actress, is accused of selling a little girl of 10 years to the Duke of Persigny ... and the great Rachel is branded a common whore.[8]

Because of the theater's supposed indecency, most people had no first hand access to it. No one saw real backstage scenes, real rehearsals, or shabby green rooms. Pictures of languid nymphs reclining on sofas and staring boldly into cameras formed the impressions of the average person. All most Victorians knew of the theater was mystery and illusion. Pornography filled in the blanks and the theater, despite the efforts of its reformers, did nothing that could counteract this view of theater as carnal and debased.

Because of the air of impropriety and mystery about them, actors and actresses were perfect subjects to become nameless, faceless, interchangeable objects of desire. Pornography about the theater gained strength by basing characters and situations in part on the real lives of real men and women, but felt no obligation to adhere only to factual information about them. However, real actors and actresses had to deal with the allegations against them in the popular imagination as if such speculation were factual. Often they replied to such charges in their autobiographies. In hers, American actress Rose Eytinge proclaimed that she never "suffered any of those perils and temptations which, we are told, beset the paths of girls who adopt the stage as a profession."[9] Ada Reeves, one of the famous Gaiety Girls, insisted that "there was little immorality among the much-maligned Chorus Ladies" despite the fact she acknowledged receiving diamond bracelets, necklaces, and "yes! even a diamond tiara." Reeves maintained that there "never was any question of a 'payment in kind'."[10] Constance Collier defended the ladies of the chorus, saying that each one seemed to have some obligation to fulfill—a sister to take care of or some pensioner to keep. She attested that these theatrical women had wonderful manners; they did not smoke or drink or swear. She found it no wonder that so many of them married into the aristocracy as "if Nature were fortifying herself and using the blood and strength of these magnificent plebeians to build a finer race."[11]

Theatrical life did have its portion of glamour and potential for exciting and profitable sexual liaisons. However, we must read these protestations that life in the chorus was like life in a nunnery bearing in mind that even more than the featured actresses, these ladies of the chorus were eroticized in pornography and the public imagination. On stage, their appearance was exotic and attractive—if somewhat faceless and interchangeable. Their demeanor seemed pliant and willing. In other words, these lovely and anonymous women moving in obedient synchronization were perfect props for a type of sexual fantasy that involved a maximization of control over one's partner and no responsibility for any consequences. In their short skirts, working for pennies, these women seemed willing to expose themselves to the gaze and control of men. Even if the average citizen could accept personal ambition for success as the motivation for a woman's pursuit of a theatrical career, that citizen would not approve of such a choice. To the Victorians, therefore, it seemed much more logical that these women who opted to appear on stage were at heart golddiggers or nymphomaniacs.

In the public imagination, ballet girls and ladies of the chorus were the perfect victims of their own greed and sex drives. This belief is evident in the rather ghoulish fascination the Victorians seemed to have with the accidental death of such young ladies in professionally related incidents. For example, because the crinolines were made of horsehair and most lighting was done by gas, many women died as a result of their large, cumbersome skirts catching on fire. This hazard was so prevalent that French fashion leader Empress Eugenie (wife of Napoleon III) publicly forsook the wearing of crinolines in order to curtail this type of tragedy. To Victorian minds, it may have seemed lamentable but inevitable poetic justice that these girls drawn to the "fatal flame" of the stage died fiery deaths. Ballet girls burned for having "burned" with sexuality.

In pornography, this justice is expressed less poetically. Take for example this summary of the pornographic novel *Memoirs of a Russian Ballet Girl*, published at the turn of the century:

> [The book] chronicles the life of Mariska, a serf born into a household of aristocrats that spank, whip, and birch all the servants from a very young age. After being apprenticed into a dressmakers' and witnessing the flagellations in the 'House of Corrections' associated with that establishment, Mariska is sent to an orphan's asylum that functions as a juvenile brothel. Finally, at the age of fifteen, she is sold into a Grand Duke's dancing academy. The fitting of her costume (tights that will split at the rear when she bends, a stiff skirt, and a bodice revealing three quarters of her large breasts) takes an entire chapter. The academy's rehearsals are open to aristocratic spectators; here the dancers wear bodices entirely revealing the bosom, very stiff short skirts, and silk stockings arranged so the thighs and buttocks are mostly bare. Corporal punishment is meted out by the ballet master during private lessons, while public

whippings always follow rehearsal and performances; the whipped girls then disappear for a few hours or overnight in the company of the courtiers. During such absences, Mariska acquires a reputation for being sexually responsive during foreplay and penetration, so she is much in demand. At the age of twenty-one, Mariska's contract expires and she is sold as a concubine to an old man who makes money by letting out his regiment of ballet girls (including ten-to-twelve-year-olds, whom he requires to fellate him before he sodomizes them) to theaters that cannot afford a regular troupe. Mariska is finally bought by a Captain of the Guards, to whom she is a willing sexual slave until her liberation.[12]

To the pornographic imagination, all ballet girls were potentially willing victims like the fictional Mariska. Such stories supplied Victorian consumers with what were, for them, logical motivations for young women to defy social norms by appearing on the public stage. Such young women, the popular mind reasoned, were victims either of unscrupulous others or of their own lusts. Pornography preferred to dwell on the latter possibility.

Pornography also victimized featured actresses. In addition to anonymous fictionalized versions of their class in pornography, they had to contend with pornographized versions of themselves that used their real names and events from their lives. It started obliquely enough. The first known serial devoted to the link between theater and pornography, the *Crim. Con. Gazette* (the title refers to a euphemism for adultery) from 1838-40, presented biographical sketches of actresses specializing in the so-called "breeches roles" (in which women played traditionally male roles) or those actresses rumored to be involved in affairs with notable men side by side with risqué stories and illustrations.[13] Such juxtaposition created an implicit link between sexual misconduct and sexual fantasy.

During their lifetimes, however, Victorian actresses writing their life stories either had to reify or try to undermine this popular image of the actress as libertine. Many, like Mowatt herself, attempted to change the public's mind. After all, it was not just their immediate reputation among their peers that was at stake, but their image for posterity. Not even theatrical historians were immune from this popular prejudice. Theater history was often the relation of unverified anecdotes by men for the enjoyment of men. In this cavalier fashion of history writing, the reputed sexual record of the actress was as pertinent as her critical reception. As quickly as such chroniclers labeled a promiscuous actress a whore, they also implied that the actress with a chaste reputation was frigid or a lesbian.

Some actresses decided that if they could not silence their critics, they could at least profit by exploiting the public's sordid expectations. For instance, in her autobiography, *Memoirs of the Life of Mrs. Sumbel, late Wells* (3 vols.; London: C. Chapple, 1811), Mary Wells presented herself as a theatrical Moll Flanders. Her story, with its "checquered passage" of "our heroine" through adventures, distresses, intimacies, persecutions, seductions, criminal prosecutions, and imprisonment, realized all of the defining traits of a picaresque novel. *Narrative of the Life of Mrs. Charlotte Clarke* (1755) is another example of a popular autobiography that provided the reading audience with a familiar narrative version of the adventures of an outcast woman.

The public craved a confirmation of its most lurid suspicions. In satisfying them, women like Mrs. Sumbel blurred the line between reality and pornographic fantasy. In opposition to the pious protestations of her sisters in the profession, in this case the actress herself wrote her life story in the style of a pornographic novel. She may have done so for many reasons. Perhaps the events of her life factually presented simply fit into this sort of titillating picaresque form. On the other hand, such a text could have been an instance of a clever woman realizing that she had no reputation to lose and a lot to gain from writing in a popular, appealing, and sensationalized style in order to make money.

Into this breech between the public theater and public decency came Anna Cora Mowatt - genteel public reader, respected authoress of the first American comedy *Fashion*, successful actress for nine years and most remarkably of all a *lady*. Her well-received biography in 1854 was a testament to her unbesmirched reputation. In 1856, she published a collection of three long stories in an anthology called *Mimic Life*. This time she seemed to be trying to save the reputation of the rest of the theatrical world, or as she put it:

> To record the singular incidents that occurred around me, and sketch the striking histories which awakened my interest, was a favorite employment during a professional career of nine years. Out of the many-colored webs of life thus collected the narratives that compose this volume are woven. Fiction has lent but a few embellishing touches. Truth is left to proclaim her own strangeness. Should this work achieve the objective contemplated, its readers will receive a more correct impression of some unlaurelled laborers for the public amusement than is generally entertained. Between them and the every-day world the curtain of prejudice has fallen in impenetrable folds. From its fatal shadow those alone who climb to the highest pinnacles of fame emerge. Yet among the most lowly of the proscribed band there are many whose lives bear witness that Heaven plants its flowers and scatters its pearls in unexpected places. Look for them, you who judge rashly, before you pronounce that they have no existence there![14]

Mowatt was responding directly to the salacious views of the theater world vividly presented in books like *Queens of the Stage: A Record of Carnal Intimacies with some of the Greatest Actresses, French, English, and German Now Living* when she wrote,

> The woman who, on the stage, is in danger of losing the highest attribute of her womanhood,—her priceless, native dower of chastity,—would be in peril of that loss in any situation of life where she was in some degree of freedom, particularly one in which she was compelled by circumstances to earn her own livelihood. I make this assertion fearlessly, for I believe it firmly. There is nothing in the profession necessarily demoralizing or degrading, not even to the poor ballet girl.[15]

This quote is one of the few times that Mowatt spoke about sex in a direct enough manner to permit a modern reader to decipher without aid of a lexicon. She put her dainty toe over the borders of propriety only for the most compelling of reasons. The misconception of the theater as a temple of carnal impropriety was a cultural wrong she believed her testimony could reverse.

Mowatt herself had shared such prejudicial views as a child. Her vision of the theater as being fantastically and corruptingly sensual had come from a minister. Once exposed to the reality of the theater in the form of a Fanny Kemble production of the popular melodrama "The Hunchback," she lost her fear of the theatrical. In much the same way, she hoped to cure her audience of its ignorant fears by exposing them in *Mimic Life* to the mundane realities of theatrical life, presenting theatrical people as ordinary mortals with the same problems and temptations. She went further to assert that the best and brightest sort of people could be found amongst the theatrical folk.

Mowatt often stated that she considered this work of fiction autobiographical. *Mimic Life* therefore can be interpreted as a continuation of her project of telling her own life story. Despite having already written an autobiography two years earlier, when writing *Mimic Life* as fiction Mowatt may have felt more free to express not simply what happened and how her encounters with others transpired, but what they meant or caused her to believe.

Throughout the book, *Mimic Life* stands in sharp contrast to the view of theater popularly held in that day. Victorians saw the theater as base and sensual, a profession that was not really a profession, a front for loafers, and a corrupter of innocents. Mowatt challenged that view through these sketches that give a more realistic view of theater as a business. Like any other business, it had its inequities and corruptions. In Mowatt's portrayal, these flaws were more often economic than carnal in origin. However, if her purpose was reforming the views of ordinary people towards the theater, she may have undermined her own cause by not being satisfied with purely mundane and factual representation of the people and situations she encountered. Although Mowatt seemingly set out to de-eroticize theater, she ended up mystifying it further by going too far in the other direction. By encoding the theater as a place of spiritual rather than sensual pain and delight, Mowatt ultimately subverted her goal of re-integrating the dramatic community into mainstream life. In her own way, she is guilty of painting as slanted and unrealistic a picture of this world as exists in the pornography written by her contemporaries.

In the same way that pornography cast the actress or the ballet girl as the victim of her own desires in order to place her further outside of society, Mowatt made her fictional actresses victims in order to make them more acceptable to society.

Apparently even Mowatt, despite her experience with the theatrical world, was still too much the Victorian lady simply to let those people work there purely because they wished to. Even for her there had to be some compelling reason why a worthy soul would venture into a workplace renowned for its corruption. Therefore her heroes and heroines were victims. These noble creatures were victims not of lust, but of circumstance.

Several of the "good" theatrical people in her stories are forced into the profession by financial misfortune. Mowatt herself became a public reader in an attempt to recoup some of the money she and her husband lost when he lost his eyesight and could no longer function as a lawyer. She gave Stella Rosenvelt, the teenaged heroine of the story that bears her name, a similar motivation. Stella's father dies before the opening pages of the story and the creditors have claimed the family's savings. Stella's mother, still in a state of shock, is unable to dissuade her daughter from a youthful plan to rescue her family from destitution by launching what Stella believes will be a lucrative stage career.

Note the similarities between the following scene in which Stella defends her decision to enter the acting profession to her prospective voice coach and the scene (quoted in chapter three) Mowatt reported in her autobiography in which she announces her resolve to go on stage to her sister May:

> Stella interrupted him impatiently: "Do not talk to me of difficulties and obstacles! Every pursuit in life has its difficulties and obstacles. Leave me to wage war with those! Will you help me? Will you fit me for what I am about to undertake? Do not refuse! I should only make the attempt without you, and then I might fail!"
>
> "If you really persist in venturing, let me caution you —"

"No, do not damp my ardor with wet-blanket cautions! I dare say I shall encounter remonstrances enough; so I make my declaration of independence at once, and give you fair warning that I shall listen to no one, since my mother has yielded her opposition."[16]

Despite the fact that her own life story was strikingly similar, Mowatt repeatedly emphasized in the narrative that Stella's embarkation on a stage career was the dangerously hare-brained and ill-considered plan of a starry-eyed adolescent.

Two of the characters Mowatt presents as male authority figures in this story are initially against Stella's plan. The first is Mr. Oakland, whom Stella is arguing with in the above passage:

Mr. Oakland, while he enjoyed to the highest degree the displays of dramatic genius,—while the performances of Siddons and O'Neill, Kemble and Cook, were engraven on tablets of steel, and treasured in his memory,—yet entertained a deep-rooted repugnance for the theatrical profession itself. Stella was aware of this antipathy, and felt sure that he would attempt to dissuade her from her purpose; but the wayward girl was too strongly armed in her self-will to believe that she could be conquered.[17]

The young would-be actress also overcomes the objections of Mowatt's second male authority figure, Stella's brother, Ernest Rosenvelt, who is himself a professional actor. When informed of her plans, he writes the following dissuasive letter:

I took a day to reflect upon your letter, and the

delay has not altered my first conviction. Stella, you well know that I reverence the profession which I adopted from choice. I toil in it with delight; I glory in the rough road over which, step by step, I may climb to eminence. You also know that I look upon none of the world's baseless prejudices as more false, more vulgar, than that which presupposes that a woman who enters this profession hazards her spotless character, or is even subjected to more than ordinary temptations. If the lode-star of purity dwell in her heart, it attracts to itself only that which is pure. If light thoughts inhabit there, and evil passions convulse her breast, then may the stage prove perilous. What place is safe to such infected blood?

Many unfortunates have brought their frailties here, and thus desecrated our temples of art; but I do not believe that through the consequences of the profession one chaste woman ever fell! For you, my sister, whose mind has been precept-strengthened and whose spirit is "in strong proof of chastity well armed," I should have no fears of shoals and quicksand. But, to launch you upon this life of turmoil, contention, perpetual struggling!—you, my delicately-natured, sensitive, excitable sister! Heaven forbid! To bid you, who have been environed, from your cradle, with the appliances of ease and opulence, exist upon the capricious breath, the uncertain suffrages, of the public?—never! To throw you with a nervous system so highly strung that its chords can be played upon by every chance breeze into this whirlwind of excitement!—never! I implore you to abandon all thoughts of the stage as a profession. Your talents may qualify you for its adoption; your temperament and education do not. The sense of fitness produced by the former is neutralized by the latter.[18]

Ignoring both men's warnings, Stella ultimately becomes the victim of her own good intentions and a lack of supervision by responsible adults.

The story seems like a negative commentary on Mowatt's own career, which began when she was only slightly older than Stella. Mowatt embarked on her career on the public stage with the full knowledge and consent of the men serving as her adult supervisors, her father and husband, both many years her senior. Despite the fact that she never questioned their wisdom in her autobiography, "Stella" seems to reprove them as irresponsible.

The heroines of the remaining two stories, "The Prompter's Daughter" and "The Unknown Tragedian," live a theatrical life out of an obligation to their parents. Tiny Tina Trueheart and Elma Ruthven are born into the theater. Mowatt introduced Tina as a baby sleeping in a stage cradle in the property room.

> But in that opposite corner—that less cumbered, well-shaded nook—how strangely unsuited to the place seem the objects there! A cradle, carefully curtained, stands alone,—a "property cradle," it is true; but the tiny form within, the little white arm thrown over the baby head, those slightly-parted lips, those closed eyes, with their deep fringes lying on the soft cheek,—are those also the crafty handiwork of the theatrical property-man?[19]

Mowatt made it ambiguous whether or not Tina is a real child or just a theatrical prop. Mowatt repeated this image of the child as object several times throughout the story. Because of the unscrupulousness of the manager they work for, Tina's poor but honest parents cannot afford to leave their work in the theater even if they wish to. Mowatt frequently pointed up the pathos of this penniless child appearing in stage costumes that make her appear rich. The Trueheart family are all victims. Her father is a hunchback who works as a prompter and her mother is a bit player. Not only are they vulnerable to the machinations of the uncaring theater manager, but they also suffer from the prejudice of society. They are characterized as decent, caring, church-going people, but Mowatt made it clear that even if they did ever manage to get enough money to escape their servitude to the theater, they would not be accepted by society at large because of that association.

Embodying this unreflective anti-theatrical bias is Miss Amory, Tina's Sunday School teacher:

> The child became a great favorite with Miss Amory; but the latter knew nothing of Tina's history. A theater the young Sunday-school teacher had never entered. She had adopted the social fiction—had become the dupe of that ignorant prejudice which caused her to look upon the temple of dramatic art with a half species of horror. She entertained a mysterious sort of belief that a theater was some "dreadful place," replete with baneful influences; that none but worthless people found employment there. A theater, and the angelic-looking child over whose spirituality, gentleness, and intellectual brilliancy, she had so often wondered, were never associated in her mind. But it was not possible for this state of things to last.[20]

On the very next page, in fact, Mowatt had little Tina confront anti-theatrical prejudice, first in the form of a snub from a classmate then with her Sunday School teacher's distaste:

"I did not know that I had been associating with an actress, Miss Tina Trueheart, and I would not demean myself by sitting beside an actress' daughter."

"An actress!" exclaimed the young teacher.

"An actress!" echoed several of the elder scholars.

"Yes, an actress!" replied Miss Haughtonville. "I saw her on the stage, myself, last Friday night, all dressed out in gauze and spangles; and I saw her mother too! They're both actresses! It's perfectly shocking to think of her being here associating with us!"

Tina's very pulses seemed suspended, so great was her amazement. She sat staring at Miss Haughtonville as though some waking nightmare possessed her. No one spoke. When her power of utterance returned, she bent towards her teacher, and gasped out, "Shocking! What does she mean!"

Miss Amory was so startled at the sudden revelation that she quite forgot the child's possible sensations, and could only say, in a deprecatory tone, "It's not true! You don't belong to such a shocking place as the theater?"[21]

In response to this incident, Mowatt put the following defense in the mouth of Tina's father:

"I don't know how I can make you understand this clearly, precious birdie; but to theaters there have sometimes belonged bad persons, bad men and women, who were actors and actresses, and their sinfulness was made known to the world. Generally it was exaggerated, and believed to be far greater than it was; and so it came about that some people are prone to think that everyone belonging to the theater is degraded. But it is not so, my child; we have among us—as the annals of crime show that other professions (even the highest, the ministry of God itself) have— unprincipled and wicked people; but we have true, honest, God-fearing people also. When you hear any one say other wise think of your dear mother"—and he pressed Susan's arm as on that day when he promised to be all to her,—"and remember that what the world thinks cannot harm you. It is what the Lord thinks,—the Lord, who sees your heart, your actions and intentions,—what He thinks alone has true importance."[23]

Despite their faith and goodness, however, the Truehearts are helpless to defend themselves against the evil and prejudice of their contemporaries.

Elma Ruthven's family is more fortunate. Her mother and father are established actors. Her mother specializes in old women and her father plays villains. The elder Ruthvens are two of the only leading characters in *Mimic Life* who continue to work in the theater because they love the life. Elma, being the decent, upright and mature Mowatt heroine that she is, dislikes being on stage. As Mowatt described her:

She shrank from the display of her talents to the incongruous crowd. She felt humiliated when she reflected that the privilege of gazing on her face, passing judgments on her endowments could be purchased.[23]

Note the sexual connotations that slip into Mowatt's

description of Elma's "instinctive" display of the conventional Victorian distaste for public display. Her parents, perhaps because of their advanced age or because they are too far outside of society to recognize these yearnings for the "normal" life in their daughter, dismiss Elma's dislike of the theater as a pretense. Not only do they urge her to stay in the theater, but they wish her to marry an actor, an action that would doom her to an inescapable life of theatricality. This unwanted marriage is the root of all the troubles for the Ruthven family in their story. If Elma were free to do as she wished (she wished to marry a young, well-connected clergyman), then there would be no conflict. In other words, if Elma were not a victim, there would be no story.

Despite Mowatt's championing of the theater, she (like pornography about the theater) could not supply her audience with a logical and believable motivation for sympathetic characters to be involved in this outcast lifestyle that does not involve victimage of some sort. She doubtlessly knew many people like the fictional Ruthvens who chose a theatrical life even while not spurred by "necessity's sharp pinch."[24] But she was too much a part of the conventional Victorian mindset to make their motivations which she vaguely described as "allurements to their minds which few considerations could compel them to resist"[25] believable to her audience and perhaps even to herself. Her true message seems to be that good souls may exist in the theater, but they are there only because they are forced to be there. Ultimately a good person cannot prosper in a world so far outside society.

I find the most disturbing aspect of Mowatt's *Mimic Life* to be that she consigns all her brightest characters to death in the end. The brilliant ingénue Stella, who much resembles a young Anna Cora Mowatt, goes insane from the strain of mastering too many roles too quickly and expires from what the physician in the story calls "a brain fever produced by injudicious mental stimulus."[26] After lingering long enough to receive all her many friends and colleagues, Stella finally dies in the following scene:

> The terrified Ernest raised and supported [Stella]. She looked imploringly in his face and struggled to speak; but her lips moved without producing a sound. Her eyes rested, with a look of love unutterable, upon every countenance in turn; fainter and fainter grew her breathing; more and more glassy became her distended orbs; and now the heavy lids drooped slowly over them. Never more would those eyes be dazzled by the glare of stage-lights; never more would that stilled heart swell or sink at the world's applause or blame. The meteor, which flashed its resplendent lustre for a moment athwart the dramatic horizon, moved in a heavenlier sphere![27]

Leaving her deathbed, Stella's survivors find the young actress's volume of Shakespeare open to the last scene of *Romeo and Juliet*. Mowatt ends the story with the following quote:

> Heaven and yourself
> Had part in this fair maid; now Heaven hath all,
> And all the better is it for the maid.
> Your part in her you could not keep from death;
> But Heaven keeps his part in eternal life!
> The most you sought was her promotion,
> And 't was your heaven she should be advanced:
> And weep ye now, seeing she is advanced
> Above the clouds, as high as heaven itself?
> O, in this love you love your child so ill,
> That you run mad, seeing that she is well![28]

These lines from the play in which she had her greatest triumph on stage serve as an epitaph for Stella.

Child prodigy Tina Trueheart dies of burns she gets while playing Ariel in Shakespere's *Tempest*. Mowatt chose the moment of Tina's highest professional achievement for her fiery accident:

There is a slight transposition of the original passages to give the performer a few moments to prepare for her aerial traveling. The time allowed is very short. After her exit, Tina bounded up the ladder, closely followed by her watchful mother. Susan had never felt prouder, more exulting, more hopeful, in her life. Alas for such moments in the human heart! Mr. Gildersleaf was standing on the platform. He carefully adjusted the wires to Tina's waist and shoulders, and tested their strength; then gave a signal to the carpenters above. The pulleys were drawn—Ariel appeared before the audience in mid air! The waving of those graceful arms moved the light wings, while the ransomed spirit smiled farewell to the group upon the stage. How the people cheered! Many rose from their seats and leaned forward; the delusion [sic] was so perfect it seemed as though she must be winging her flight through the atmosphere without support. The floating form was almost out of sight, when suddenly it stopped. The arms were still waved, and the light wings responded, but the figure remained immovable. The wires in some inexplicable manner had become entangled, the pulleys refused to work; the child—Heaven guard her! she was suspended immediately over one of the side-lights used to illuminate the back portion of the stage!

A heart-rending shriek, that pierced every ear, burst from Susan's lips, and gave the first announcement of the impending danger. Regardless of the audience, she dashed frantically across the stage, crying, "Cut the wires! my child, my child! she will be burned to death!"[29]

Although badly burned, Tina lingers on long enough to bring almost the entire city of London to repentance for their evil ways through her nobly-born suffering. Finally, the child dies backstage just after her mother, playing Queen Katherine's servant Patience in Shakespeare's *Henry the Eighth*, completes singing a hymn over the dead queen on stage. Father and Mother finish their professional duties in time to come backstage and sing for their dying child:

> While they still sang, a change passed over the child's countenance; paler it could not grow, but its pallor became transparent. The limbs quivered slightly, and then were extended to their utmost length; the eyes opened wide, as though they saw something invisible to others; she smiled seraphically, and then her features gradually assumed a marble-like rigidity; there was a gurgling, rattling sound in her throat, which the music did not wholly drown; the hands clasped upon her bosom slowly relaxed,—all was very still.[30]
>
> Although her father manages to survive, Tina's mother dies of grief a few pages later.

Elma Ruthven is spared, but both her parents and the young tragedian that they chose as her unsuitable suitor all expire in the course of the story. Mowatt gave Mortimer, the young tragedian, a spectacular on-stage suicide while playing Bertram in *The Tragedy of Bertram* by Rev. Charles Maturin, a role made famous by Edmund Kean:

> After the death of Imogine, instead of snatching a sword from one of the knights (according to stage

directions), he drew a dagger from his own girdle. The steel glittered for an instant, as he pronounced the words, "Bertram has but one fatal foe on earth, and he is here!" then was violently plunged into his breast. He sank upon the ground, exclaiming, in an exultant tone, "Lift up your holy hands in charity! I died no felon death—A warrior's weapon freed a warrior's soul!"

Elma's eyes were closed as she lay upon the stage. She marked not the red current that flowed upon the ground, even till it reached her white raiment. The actors beheld it, and looked aghast. The audience saw it with mute horror.

Mortimer lay motionless, weltering in blood. The curtain fell. His companions stooped to raise him.

"Gently! gently!" he groaned; "you are— carrying—a—dying—man!"

They bore him to the green-room, and laid him upon the sofa.

"Is he fatally injured?" "How came he by a sharp dagger?" "Was it an accident?" were the whispered queries of pallid lips on every side.

Elma knelt by the couch, and with firm and skillful hands essayed to bind up the wound.

He shook his head, as he regarded her, and said, hoarsely, "Past all surgery!" Then, with a painful effort, he lifted his hand, felt in his bosom, took thence a stained and crumpled paper, and thrust it into her hands.

His voice was so faint that she could scarcely distinguish his words (so she bore testimony afterwards), but she thought they were, "It is annulled; let the sacrifice not be in vain! Pardon, O, my God! Pardon, for her sake!"

A portion of the audience had rushed behind the scenes, and now thronged the apartment. From their midst, Mr. Ruthven pressed forward, with tottering limbs and horror-stricken countenance. When he saw Elma bending over Mortimer, with crimsoned hands and garments, he would have fallen, had not a manly arm supported him. It was that of Edmonton.

Mortimer's glazing eyes turned to his aged friend, and to him by whose arm he was sustained. He motioned them to draw near. The old man appeared stupefied by grief. He seemed incapable of obeying Mortimer's gesture. It supplicated him to bend down, that he might catch the words the dying man could with difficulty articulate. But Edmonton bowed his head close to the pale and stiffening lips.

When he raised his face again, Mortimer had expired.[31]

Elma probably survives only because she gives up the theater and marries Edmonton, a parson. By the story's logic, Mortimer's sacrificial death makes this course possible as the following excerpt explains:

Since Mortimer's tragical death Mr. Ruthven's mind was gradually weaned from its fondness for the stage. He had slowly consented to Elma's casting off the glittering chain that had long pressed heavily on her unambitious, unworldly heart.[32]

Elma Ruthven, thus, is spared a painful physical death, but does experience a soul-ordering transition ritual of a similar sort as she makes her farewell tour and leaves the stage. She dies figuratively rather than literally to the world of the stage and ends her story much as Tina and Stella exited theirs, joined to a religious ideal with a serene smile on her face.

In Mowatt's book, the character who exhibits dramatic genius inevitably surrenders completely to his/her characterizations, becomes unable to function in the "normal" world, and dies. This carnage is unsettling in a work that its author called autobiographical. The offstage agony of the most talented of Mowatt's artists grows in direct proportion to their onstage triumph. It seems almost a relief for them to die. What does this suffering and death mean coming from a woman who was a popular and critical success as an actress?

To understand the torment of Mowatt's antagonists, one must appreciate the Victorian distaste and fear of metamorphosis. The fear of continually becoming is crystallized in the horror novels of the period like Bram Stoker's classic, *Dracula*. The prevalent Victorian belief that an individual could change or be changed radically had both positive and negative connotations. Reformers and crusaders of the period like Dorthea Dix and Brigham Young personify the belief that humanity could evolve into an improved form. Fictive monsters like Dracula embody the fear of constant mutation that never ends in an achieved identity. Michael Wheeler summarized this dark side of the evolving self in his book *Death and the Future Life in Victorian Literature*:

> The Victorian self refuses to stop becoming; its development produces only spectacular trans-formations. Its theatrical, incessant, and perhaps uncontainable energies draw it toward the death that might give it rest.[33]

The theater, as Wheeler indicated, was a perfect metaphor for a continual, unsettling state of metamorphosis. Such a state was so repugnant that even the "liberal" folks of the theater took steps to protect their actresses from this danger. The practice of type casting limits the range of transformation the player must achieve. As John Elsom points out, women's roles usually highlighted a single attitude such as nobility, innocence, or diabolism rather than demand that the actress display the startling versatility expected of a male leading player such as Henry Irving.[34]

Theatrical metamorphosis was manifest in the short life of Tina Trueheart. Unlike a mature actress, she was required to display her talent for transforming into anyone of either gender. The role furthermost from Tina's natural state was Ariel, from Shakespeare's Tempest. Mowatt described her in costume:

> The fair, fragile child, in her gossamer robe, looped here and there with sprays of bright sea-weed; with her shining, filmy wings: her floating hair interwound with branches of white and scarlet coral: her girdle and bracelets of shells: looked the island sprite indeed,—a being scarce earthly![35]

Ariel was also Tina's last role. Her fatal accident took place while portraying the sprite. Perhaps Shakepeare's unreal, sexless creature marked the outer boundaries of theatrical transformation for Mowatt. By Tina Trueheart's molding of herself to resemble this fantastic creature, the child demonstrates a limitless capacity to mimic any creation the imagination of man might dream up.

Mowatt's Stella suffers a complete nervous and physical breakdown after perfecting impersonations of Pauline (from *Lady of Lyons*), Virginia (*Virginius*), Evadne (*Evadne*), Desdemona (*Othello*), Beatrix (*Much Ado About Nothing*), Juliet (*Romeo and Juliet*), and Ophelia (*Hamlet*) in quick succession. With each metamorphosis, the real Stella becomes more obscured as is foreshadowed in the following description of the ingénue after rehearsing the role of Juliet:

While she was making her toilet, she caught sight of her own countenance in the mirror just as she again unconsciously uttered that frantic ejaculation. She gazed in wonder at the haggard, terrified expression, and then laughed to see the look change to one of surprise. It seemed to her as if she were scanning the face of another. She was indeed "losing her own identity."[36]

As she described the young actress's impersonation of Ophelia, Mowatt completely blurred the line between character and actress:

When Stella appeared upon the stage in the fourth act,—her hair unbound and disheveled, her eyes dilated until they appeared of the jettiest black, and luminous with the peculiar light of insanity, her white drapery disordered, her movements rapid and uncertain,—her personation of the distraught Ophelia became painfully real.[37]

As an adolescent, Stella's personality is established firmly enough that this loss of self is sufficiently disturbing to drive her insane in this fiction.

However, even in Mowatt's fictive world of fragile-minded Victorian women, Tina Trueheart could not find refuge in a mental retreat from reality. This little girl had been raised in the theater. She was playing roles before she could speak. Tina never has the chance to form a stable, conventionally Victorian self-concept. If Tina had not died, the child prodigy would have been doomed to a life of constant metamorphosis. She would have lived in a constant flux, always exploited for her ability to assume personalities other than her own. Though bringing happiness to others and monetary success to her parents, Tina's life is a tragedy of selflessness. Constant metamorphosis was a fate worse than death.

Stella and Tina were not living healthy, normal, real lives in Mowatt's estimation, but rather only mimic lives as the author warned us in her title. As an alternative to prolonging this cruel existence, Anna Cora Mowatt did the humane thing as author and killed her characters. Nina Auerbach claimed that in Victorian literature women's conversions are nullified by marriage or death.[38] In *Mimic Life*, Stella, Tina Trueheart, and even the reluctant Elma Ruthven are caught up in lives of constant metamorphosis.

An individual could never reach the Victorian ideal of noble existence if he/she could not reach an end of changing and mutating. Conventional Victorians seemed to want their lives to fade into the sort of neat, "happily ever after" sort of closure that much of their fiction did. However life's unpredictability frustrated that desire. Perhaps this dread of metamorphosis caused Mowatt to connect theatrical life with insanity. To be caught in a life that demanded that one change and transform nightly goes completely against a desire for stability and closure. Individuals who chose a theatrical life even denied themselves the privacy that conventional Victorians cherished. On stage, one metamorphosized on display like a freak.

For women, particularly, the achievement of noble stability was problematic. The testimony of Victorian fiction seems to indicate that women could only achieve this valorized state through the resolution of death. Wheeler feels that the longing for death's cohering touch explains the embarrassing eroticism of so many Victorian deathbeds for female characters:

Dicken's Little Nell, Emily Bronte's Catherine,
Robert Browning's Pompila, all become, in their
lingering, lushly orchestrated deaths, aroused centers
of desire. For all, the consummation that proved

elusive in life explodes at life's end. The erotic female corpses, or near-corpses, with which so many Victorian paintings are decorated—Rossetti's Beata Beatrix and Millais' drowning Ophelia are orgiastically convulsed by death's approach—appear perverse or offensive in the necrophilic abandon they inspire. However, they represent something more affirmative than a sinister fondness for dead women: these aroused corpses stimulate in the viewer pride of life only death offers.[39]

Women were, in short, better off dead.

To the Victorians, death was not ultimately a negative experience. Death was not the existential horror of incomprehensible non-existence that many perceive it as today. In death, one changed no more. One achieved a purity and went on to eternal, conflict-free stability - be it pleasant or unpleasant. Rape or defilement placed one irreversibly on the road of unpredictability, outside society and subject to the buffets of unkind fate. This permanent sentence to a life of instability was a terrible fate for women who were believed to be naturally unstable and inconsistent, unable by their very nature to achieve stability except in the most protected environments. The perfect death was a final triumph of the spirit over the body. All the elements had to be in place, not just for public show, but to satisfy the deep Victorian longing for closure. Death was showy and public. It was essentially theatrical, but a theatricality boiled clean of any hint of overt sexuality. Unlike theater, the metamorphosis of the corpse to spirit in the Victorian spectacle of the funeral was predictable and ordered. Death was everything that life was not.

Anna Cora Mowatt was a firm believer in such a concept of a static, family-oriented afterlife. After a strange experience with mesmerism during a long illness, she became a devout follower of Emmanuel Swedenborg, a leading propagator of

Victorian visions of a bourgeois heaven. Death was celebrated, not mourned by members of Swedenborg's New Church because it so outshone the trials of mortal life. Therefore when Anna Cora Mowatt killed off her characters, she did so as if giving them a beautiful gift. Good characters in *Mimic Life* have lavishly described deaths that closely adhere to the general outlines of the ideal Victorian death. Life on Earth could only mean more pain for her actor/characters, pain intensified, not relieved by success in their chosen careers. One wonders if Mowatt herself longed for the cleansing deaths she gave her heroines and heroes.

Sometimes in as in the case of the flammable ballet girls, the popular view of theatrical women also consigned them to death. More often than not in pornography of the theater, theatrical women, like the much-abused ballet girl Mariska, wind up in a sexual never-never land in almost fairy-tale "happily ever after" type endings. Characters exist not in the real world but in what Steven Marcus calls a "pornuptopia,"[40] a placeless place, an upside-down version of Victorian reality where the sexuality normally forbidden is permissible and normal.

Both the pornographers and Anna Cora Mowatt—no matter the amount of gritty reality they used to tell their stories—consigned their characters to unreal places when deciding their ultimate fates. Both Mowatt's characters' highly aestheticized heaven and Mariska's Russian pornutopia are imaginary sites where characters slip from this world of stress and pain into a perfectly ordered society of like-minded people.

In *Mimic Life*, Mowatt both reified and contradicted the popular view of Theater. She created theatrical characters that are sympathetic in defiance of the common perception that such persons were either drawn to the Theater by their base desires or inevitably corrupted by life in the Theater. However she echoed the grave warnings of those biased against the Theater in her often tragic plots. Mowatt stayed just far enough within conventional narrative strategies and conventional morality to maintain narrative authority. *Mimic Life* maintains the delicate balance necessary for Mowatt to speak to a conventional Victorian audience in defense of her chosen profession and her constructed public self.

CHAPTER 5

FEAR, LOATHING, AND FASHION:
SELF-CREATION IN ANNA CORA MOWATT'S DRAMA

As an unknown, female, American dramatic author writing in the 1840's, Anna Cora Mowatt had many negative preconceptions to overcome before writing a successful play. Remarkably, she achieved financial and critical success with her first attempt, a comedy called *Fashion*. In the play, she displayed an insider's knowledge of what was "in" and "out" with the well-to-do that fascinated her audiences without alienating theater patrons who actually were of that social class. Rather than simply ridiculing fashionable follies, the things that an outsider would find ridiculous, Mowatt's comedy cut to the heart of upper class discomfort with the artificiality and accessibility of fashion as a short cut to social power as well as lower and middle class discomfort with the upper class in general. In *Fashion*, Mowatt makes not only the point that fashion sometimes leads people to do things that look foolish to the uninitiated, but that the ignorant following of the forms of fashion can lead people do to things that are foolish and dangerous as well. In writing Fashion, Mowatt did more than craft a play that her audiences would enjoy. She also created a self as the implied author whom her auditors would grant the right to a public voice.

Today, Anna Cora Mowatt's comedy, *Fashion: Life in New York*, is a museum piece. Theater historians generally recognize it as the first American social comedy. The play is a half-way point on the road between Royall Tyler's *The*

Contrast, the first play to contain a character that is uniquely an "American" type, and the numerous specimens of modern, distinctly American comedy. Most modern stagings of *Fashion* have occurred in academic settings, framing Mowatt's melodrama as a representative sample of a bygone era in the evolution of American drama.[1]

Although it never achieved the notoriety or mass appeal of the dramatic adaptations of Harriet Beecher Stowe's *Uncle Tom's Cabin* (circa 1854), *Fashion* enjoyed a respectably long period of popularity from its debut in 1845 to the beginning of the Civil War. The comedy made Anna Cora Mowatt famous. Its publication marked the end of her period of writing under various pseudonyms. *Fashion* established Mowatt a place among the dramatists of America and made her a member of the New York literati. Her experiences with the production of the play also opened the way for her successful career as an actress.

Theater historian Arthur Hobson Quinn, writing in 1951, asserted that *Fashion* deserved its success for being a social satire "based on real knowledge of the life it depicts, but painting it without bitterness, without nastiness, and without affectation."[2] The comedy's weak plot to him was not important. Quinn felt Mowatt's drawing of characters gave the play a right to live.

Mowatt's delineation of characters that spoke and acted more like actual Americans than mere copies of European comic stereotypes is definitely what has secured Fashion its place in the evolution of American drama. However, I do not think this is a sufficient explanation of its popular success with audiences in the 1840's and 50's. Edgar Allan Poe, working then as drama critic for a publication called *The Broadway Journal*, reported, rather peevishly, that the play was frequently interrupted by "the clapping of hands and the rattling of canes" of audience members in what he felt was a conventionalized and predictable response to certain lines and situations.[3] What

Poe found to be unreflective and undiscriminating responses interests me. In this chapter, I would like to look at the elements of this play that made it stirringly comic for its audience.

Students of the human psyche from Freud to the present maintain that humor is a civilized mask hiding fear and hostility. I propose that Mowatt's comedy *Fashion* struck a responsive chord with her audience, despite the extratextual factors that should have predisposed a large segment of her auditors to dislike the play, because she was able to tap strong undercurrents of anxiety and anger in her audience. Her autobiography suggests that Mowatt intended this play to be both humorous and instructive for her auditors. In *Fashion*, she constructed a play that amused her listeners by exposing their frailties.

The plot of *Fashion* revolves around the woes of Mr. Tiffany, a dry-goods merchant brought to the brink of bankruptcy by his fashion-worshiping wife. Mrs. Tiffany is a former milliner who, along with her sister Prudence, sold flashy caps and hats in a little store on Canal Street. She chatters in execrable French, apes French customs, and loves unbounded pretension.

In order to pay his debts, Tiffany has forged checks in front of his private secretary, Snobson. To free himself from Snobson's power, Tiffany urges his daughter Seraphina to marry the surly clerk. Mrs. Tiffany wishes Seraphina to marry Count Jolimaitre, an imposter who is in reality a cook named Gustave Treadmill. For some time the "Count" had lived in Paris. He left hurriedly, forsaking a young girl to whom he was betrothed, who had given him all of her savings. This girl, Millinette, is now serving as maid for the Tiffanys. Also living in the house is Gertrude, a virtuous young lady who serves as music teacher for Seraphina. Colonel Howard, a U.S. Army officer, is in love with Gertrude.

Adam Trueman, a wealthy farmer from Catteraugus

county, visits his old friend, Mr. Tiffany. Trueman is shocked at the changes in the family and disgusted by Snobson's "hang-dog face." The old farmer tells Mrs. Tiffany that her fashionable ways are leading her husband down the road to ruin. Prudence, Mrs. Tiffany's sister, is attracted to the plain-spoken Trueman. She informs him that Gertrude, whom the farmer instinctively likes because of her sweet, unaffected nature, is in love with T. Tennyson Twinkle, a poet who contributes to the "New Monthly Vernal Galaxy" and claims that the true test of a poet is the velocity at which he composes. Poet Twinkle, however, is primarily interested in Seraphina Tiffany's fortune. His rival, in addition to Count Jolimaitre, is Mr. Augustus Fogg, a member of an old family, a gourmand who is bored by everything until dinner is served.

Millinette discovers the true identify of Jolimaitre. When she threatens to expose him, he convinces her that he can explain everything at supper the following Friday. Gertrude, overhearing the plans for this rendezvous, decides to take Millinette's place at the agreed upon hour in the housekeeper's room. She asks Zeke, the comic black butler, to assist her by detaining Millinette from keeping her appointment with Jolimaitre.

Prudence complicates the plot by overhearing Gertrude give these instructions to Zeke. She ruins Gertrude's plan and reputation by bringing the entire family into the room where Gertrude and Jolimaitre are meeting. Explanations are futile. Colonel Howard is so despondent he decides to resign his commission and leave the city.

Since no one in the Tiffany household will listen to her, Gertrude writes a letter to her old friends in Geneva (a small American town) explaining everything. Trueman enters while she is writing and reads the letter. From it, he discovers that Gertrude is not only innocent, but is in fact the daughter of his deceased daughter Ruth.

Strengthened by this knowledge, Trueman kicks out

Snobson, publicly claims Gertrude as his long-lost grand-daughter, arranges for Colonel Howard to marry her, and lends money to Tiffany on the condition that he send his wife and daughter to the country where they may learn native rural virtues. Trueman also promises to set up the exposed but repentant "Count" in a restaurant if he, in a cook's uniform, will solicit business from his former fashionable friends.

Trueman does not marry Prudence and Seraphina does not find a husband, but everyone else seems to be set to live happily ever after by the end of the play.

As many critics have noted, the plot is not the play's strongest or most original feature. Poe and others commented on its similarity to *School for Scandal* and other plays by Sheridan in its reliance on overheard conversations and unlikely coincidences.[4] Like Tyler's *The Contrast*, the play paints the virtue of the Yankee hero as opposed to the foreign dandy. There are also similarities between *Fashion* and Mead's *Wall Street; or, Ten Minutes Before Three* (1819) and William Dunlap's *The Father; or, American Shandy-ism* (1789). James Nelson Barker's *Tears and Smiles* (1807) was a comedy of manners set in Philadelphia. One of the characters, Fluttermore, is a fop who apes the French in manners and conversation. J.H. Hackett's *Moderns; or, A Trip to the Springs* (1831) is a satire on the caprices of a summer colony. Poe pointed out that even the name "Trueman" occurred in J.K. Paulding's *The Lion of the West* (1831), a play which featured a Canadian barber who poses as a count, a humorous and generous Kentuckian who helps to bring the plot to a happy termination by straightening the crisscross tangles, and a long-lost daughter who is found by one of the characters.

Numerous contemporary novels also had plot-situations that recall *Fashion*. For instance, Catherine M. Sedgwick's *Clarence, a Tale of Our Own Times* (1830) contains a character named Gertrude Clarence, a sensible girl who saves her friend Emilie Layton from running away with an adventurer. Gertrude

Clarence could have easily served as the original for *Fashion's* Gertrude.

Mowatt could have also gotten much of her plot from reading the current newspapers and magazines. To cite one example, in his editorial in *New World* of June 13, 1840, Park Benjamin reports the story of a student named Eldridge who had been employed and introduced into society by Dr. Mott. The young man turned out to be a forger. "Eldridge," said Benjamin, "had as legitimate a right to the houses he visited as two-thirds of the young men about town, and a far superior claim to the French barbers and German fiddlers, whose only letters of recommendation are redundant moustaches and swaggering airs of insolence."[5]

Mowatt herself stated that *Fashion* was not an attempt at what she called "fine writing." "I designed the play wholly as an acting comedy," she reported in her *Autobiography*. "A dramatic, not a literary, success was what I desired to achieve. Caution suggested my not aiming at both at once."[6]

She wrote the play during her long convalescence from the respiratory illness that resulted from the physical and emotional stresses of her brief career as a public reader. Although her readings had been well received by both critics and audiences, several of Mowatt's friends and relations strongly disapproved of her choice to go on the stage even in the relatively respectable venue of reading programs. She had turned to giving readings when her husband's illness and bad investments forced the Mowatts to the verge of bankruptcy. Despite her efforts, the couple lost Melrose, their elegant Flatbush estate. During this low period of her life, Mowatt reported that "a vein of sarcasm, developed by the trials through which I had passed, pervaded all my thoughts, and betrayed itself in much that I wrote as well as in conversation."[7] Her friend Epes Sargent suggested that she channel her bitter wit into a creative endeavor. As Mowatt described in her *Autobiography*:

E. S——-'s suggestion appeared to me good, and I commenced *Fashion*. If it is a satire on American parvenuism, it was intended to be a good humored one. No charge can be more untrue than that with which I have been taxed through the press and in private—the accusation of having held up to ridicule well-known personages. The character of Mrs. Tiffany is not drawn from any one individual, but was intended as the type of a certain class. The only character in the play which was sketched from life was that of the blunt, warm-hearted old farmer. I was told that the original was seen in the pit vociferously applauding Adam Trueman's strictures on fashionable society. It was not very wonderful that his sentiments found an echo in my friend's bosom. I longed to ask the latter whether he recognized his own portrait; but we have never met since the likeness was taken.[8]

Fashion was a tremendous hit with its tiny first audience, consisting primarily of James Mowatt, Epes Sargent and one or two other close personal friends who listened by the fireside to the playwright's rough drafts of scenes. This was also to remain Mowatt's favorite audience as she said in a letter to James Sargent, Epes' brother:

Every line and every word (of your letter)—ay, the very hand-writing itself conjured back to life those happy evenings when you and Epes, and husband, used to sit in solemn or mirthful judgment over such portions of *Fashion* as I had concocted during the morning. What delight I took in hearing you predict *Fashion's* success. Alas! the verifying of that prediction gave me more pain than pleasure. I have now seen *Fashion* so often murdered in all its minor and greater parts before a gaping throng, that the only pleasant thoughts connected with it are linked with its first perusal before my beloved fireside judges of the Fourth Avenue—which by the way is of the largest avenues laid out by memory and affection in my heart...[9]

At the urging of Sargent, Mowatt presented the complete play to Mr. Edward Simpson, manager of the Park Theater. Simpson was also a former neighbor of Anna Cora's childhood home and a long-time acquaintance. As may not have happened with manuscripts by other first-time authors, Simpson read the former Miss Ogden's play at once, decided that he liked it, passed the manuscript to Mr. Berry, the stage manager, and told him to put the play into rehearsal at once.

The cast assembled by the management of the Park for *Fashion*'s debut included several famous troupers of the American stage of that day. The cast list for the opening read as follows:

Adam Trueman	Mr. Chippendale
Count Jolimaitre	Mr. W.H. Crisp
Colonel Howard	Mr. Dyott
Mr. Tiffany	Mr. Barry
Fogg	Mr. J. Howard
Snobson	Mr. Fisher
Zeke	Mr. Skerrett
Twinkle	Mr. De Walden
Mrs. Tiffany	Mrs. Barry
Gertrude	Miss Ellis
Prudence	Mrs. Knight
Seraphina	Miss Horn
Millinette	Mrs. Dyott[10]

On the evening of March 24, 1845, *Fashion* was presented. In her *Autobiography*, Mowatt noted with amazement the transformation the theater had undergone from the dismal rehearsal she had attended the previous night. The Park was ablaze with lights, the boxes, pit, and gallery were filled with many of New York Society's "upper ten-thousand" and the musicians were playing wonderfully stirring music. The Park Theater, owned by John Jacob Astor, was the theater to many New Yorkers until the opening of Astor Place Opera House in 1848. The theater was in financial difficulties and would be destroyed by fire in 1847, but was saved temporarily by the success of *Fashion*.[11]

Despite the fact that the Park was the most splendid American theater of the early nineteenth century, it was a meager, cramped and dreary facility by later standards. The building had no lobby as such. Seven arched doorways faced Park Row. The outer two led directly up to the third tier and gallery. The middle five conveyed patrons to the two tiers of boxes and to the pit. Except for box subscriptions, seating was not reserved. Theatergoers squeezed onto benches in the pit and gallery or, for particularly popular performances, stood. The houselights remained brightly lit the entire evening.[12]

Despite the inelegant setting, the management and the patrons made *Fashion*'s opening into quite a stylish event. A. Oakley Hall, a contemporary columnist writing about *Fashion*'s debut, emphasized the pretentiousness of the whole affair. The management headed posters and bills simply "Theater" as though there were no other playhouse. Many notables of New York society were in attendance. Members of the Astor, Stuyvesant, Fish, Duyckinck, and Van Zandt families were in the boxes. Among other distinguished New Yorkers present for the opening were Mayor James Harper, Recorder Tallmadge, Judges Betts and Dent, General James Watson Webb, James Gordon Bennett, Park Godwin, Edgar Allan Poe, N.P. Willis, and Park Benjamin.[13]

When the opening music concluded, Mr. W.H. Crisp, who played Count Jolimaitre, appeared before the curtain and delivered the following prologue written by Epes Sargent:

Prologue (Enter a Gentleman, reading a newspaper.)
"Fashion, a Comedy.' I'll go; but stay —
Now I read Farther, 'tis a native play!
Bah! homemade calicoes are well enough,
But homemade drama must be stupid stuff.
Had it the London stamp, 'twould do—but then,
For plays, we lack the manners and the men!
    Thus speaks one critic. Hear another's creed;—
"'Fashion!' What's here? (reads) It never can succeed!
What! from a woman's pen? It takes a man
To write a comedy—no woman can."
    Well, sir, and what say you, and why that frown?
His eyes uprolled, he lays the paper down;—
"Here! take!," he says, "the unclean thing away!
'Tis tainted with the notice of such a play!"
    But, sir!—but gentleman!—you, sir, who think
No comedy can flow from native ink, —
Are we such perfect monsters, or such dull,
That Wit no traits for ridicule can cull?
Have we no follies here to be redressed?
No vices gibbeted? no crimes confessed?
"But then a female hand can't lay the lash on!"
How know you that, sir, when the theme is FASHION?
    And now, come forth, thou man of sanctity!
How shall I venture a reply to thee?
The Stage—what is it, though beneath thy ban,
But a daguerreotype of life and man?
Arraign poor human nature, if you will,
But let the DRAMA have her mission still;
Let her, with honest purpose, still reflect
The faults which keeneyed Satire may detect.

For there be men who fear not an hereafter,
Yet tremble at the hell of public laughter!
  Friends, from these scoffers we appeal to you!
Condemn the false, but O, applaud the true.
Grant that some wit may grow on native soil,
And Art's fair fabric rise from woman's toil.
While we exhibit but to reprehend
The social vices, 'tis for you to mend![14]

This speech was most probably in response to the following short item that appeared in *Spirit of the Times,* on March 15, 1845, under the heading "Green Room Intelligence":

"A Native Comedy" by a Mrs. Mowatt is rumored to be in rehearsal at the Park. We have little confidence in female dramatic productions of the present time, but we wish the lady a happy debut although it may be five long acts.[15]

Despite the doubts of the reviewer for *Spirit of the Times, Fashion* was an immediate success. The play ran for three weeks in New York. In Philadelphia, the Walnut Street Theater immediately assembled a cast including W. Rufus Blake, the stage manager, as Trueman, Mrs. Thayer as Prudence and Susan Cushman as Seraphina for a successful run in that city.

Mowatt sent out copies of the manuscript in advance of the production to several of the drama critics for the major newspapers. The following letter she sent to Edgar Allan Poe was probably typical of her deferential approach to her potential critics:

Edgar A. Poe, Esqr. (I regret that) I have not a more legible manuscript of the Comedy to submit to your perusal, or even one containing all the corrections made at the suggestion of critical advisers. The only fair copy is in the hands of the managers, and that I could not procure. Your criticisms will be prized—I am sorry that they could not have been made before preparations for the performance of the Comedy had progressed so far.[16]

This courtesy proved to be a wise move on her part. *Fashion*'s only completely negative review after its opening night came from the critic from *Spirit of the Times*, who not only did not seem to have received an advance copy of the script, but might not have been entirely pleased by being publicly lampooned in Epes Sargent's prologue:

> *Fashion* is a thoroughly inferior comedy, a typical product of a person who, having seen a play, immediately believes he can write one. It was a failure for the language of comedy is not the ordinary slipshod conversational stringing together of words employed in everyday life—comic writing should be terse, epigrammatic... the plot should comprise a narration of real events intermixed with others of a decidedly artificial nature, and above all, the action should be staged in the course of the piece.[17]

This reviewer had not cooled down even by April 5th, when the play was mentioned again. The critic implied that Mowatt got *Fashion* produced by "pull." To explain its success, the reviewer praised and condemned the actors in one sentence.

> After murdering some four-score pieces of standard worth, they absolutely make a comedy out of

Fashion—to the popular eyes at least. To its neatly turned points of satire, one has added a shrug of the shoulder, another a jocose leer... without the actors, *Fashion* would be intolerable.[18]

John William Stanhope Hows of the New York *Albion*, who *had* received an advance copy, was positively ebullient in his review, declaring that *Fashion* satisfactorily solved the question of there being materials in American society for constructing a successful comedy and a writer capable of adapting these materials:

> It is with no ordinary feelings of satisfaction that we record the triumphant verdict of the public in favor of Mrs. Mowatt's comedy... It has created a sensation unexampled in theatricals and has decisively established the fact that the time has arrived when a strictly American drama can be called into existence.[19]

The reviewer for the *Evening Post* pronounced the script's dialogue "sprightly" and abounding in "pertinent local and national allusions." The review went on to say that although a few of those allusions were "perhaps a little antiquated," they still had "a telling effect on the audience."[20] The reviewer for the *New York Herald* saw *Fashion* with its distinct American flavor as "a new movement not only in theatricals, but in society, manners, and literature."[21]

The most balanced view of the play came from Edgar Allan Poe, writing for *The Broadway Journal*. Poe saw *Fashion* several times during its run and wrote two lengthy reviews of it. In his first commentary, he used *Fashion* as an object lesson for dissecting the ills of contemporary drama. The play, he felt, though entertaining, was hopelessly conventional. Events had little relation to everyday reality. He wrote:

> We must say that *Fashion* is theatrical but not dramatic. It is a pretty well-arranged selection from the usual routine of stage characters, and stage maneuvers—but there is not one particle of any nature, beyond greenroom nature, about it. No such events ever happened in fact, or ever could happen, as happen in *Fashion*. Nor are we quarrelling now with the mere exaggeration of the character or incident—were this all, the play, although bad as comedy might be good as farce, of which the exaggeration of possible incongruities is the chief element. Our fault-finding is on the score of deficiency in verisimilitude—in natural art—that is to say, in art based in the natural laws of man's heart and understanding.[22]

He went on to state that his complaint was not specifically against *Fashion* in particular, but contemporary drama in general, which unlike other manifestations of Art, had not yet seemed to have advanced beyond the Renaissance.

Poe went on to praise the production's good points:

> The colloquy in Mrs. Mowatt's comedy is spirited, generally terse, and well seasoned at points with sarcasm of much power. The management throughout show the fair authoress to be thoroughly conversant with our ordinary stage effects, and we might say a good deal in commendation of some of the "sentiments" interspersed: we are really ashamed, nevertheless to record our deliberate opinion that if *Fashion* succeed at all (and we think upon the whole

that it will) it will owe the greater portion of its success to the very carpets, the very ottomans, the very chandeliers, and the very conservatories that gained so decided a popularity for the most inane and utterly despicable of all modern comedies, the *London Assurance* of Boucicault.[23]

After repeated viewing and further thought, Poe amended his evaluation of the play:

> In one respect, perhaps, we have done Mrs. Mowatt unintentional injustice. We are not quite sure, upon reflection, that her entire thesis is not an original one. We can call to mind no drama, just now, in which the design can be properly stated as the satirizing of fashion as fashion. Fashionable follies, indeed, as a class of folly in general, have been frequently made the subject of dramatic ridicule—but the distinction is obvious—although certainly too nice a one to be of any practical avail to the authoress of a new comedy.[24]

The distinction that Poe found obvious, Mowatt's satirizing fashion as fashion instead of the more common practice of ridiculing fashionable foibles, is one on which I wish to focus. To understand this distinction, one must first examine what Poe and Mowatt were including under the rubric of "fashion." Here is one definition from the lips of Mowatt's characters:

> Trueman: Fashion! And pray what is fashion, madam? An agreement between certain persons to live without using their souls! to substitute etiquette for

> virtue—decorum for purity - manners for morals! to affect a shame for the works of their Creator! and expend all their rapture upon the works of their tailors and dressmakers!
>
> Mrs. Tiffany: You have the most ow-tray ideas, Mr. Trueman—quite rustic, and deplorably American![25]

The word fashion here is being used not to indicate simply clothing, stylishness, etiquette, or trendiness, but rather the self-conscious construction of a public image demanding respectability through the indication of material success.

Revolutions in both America and Europe de-legitimated the distinctions of birth as a method of measuring the worth of men and women, giving the growing American middle and lower classes unparalleled opportunity to claim for themselves privileges and power previously out of their reach. They soon found out, though, that just being able to pay the price of admission did not guarantee acceptance into the exclusive circles of social privilege. Despite the aggressive egalitarianism of the Age of Jackson, an aspirant to the highest levels of respectability had to distinguish him/herself from the democratic mob. One of the most important ways that one separated oneself from the unwashed was to behave like a "lady" or a "gentleman."

In 19th century America these terms acquired a new meaning quite different from the connotations in preceding ages. According to etiquette manuals of the time, a "lady" or "gentleman" was not necessarily an aristocrat, nor a plutocrat. Such "aristocrats of nature" recognized a gulf between themselves and people in trade. They went to pains to do nothing that would lessen this distinction, but they did not deny the gap between themselves and the aristocracy. They claimed certain affinities with the latter and none with the former. Their peculiar mental outlook was similar to, if not identical with that of "the Best People." The new definition for the traditionally aristocratic European titles of "lady" and "gentlemen" did not involve being born into an aristocratic European family (although noble birth never hurt). The previously synonymous terms of "Gentlewoman" and "Lady" were now separate. A "Gentlewoman," claimed etiquette authors of the 1840s, was born so, a "Lady," on the other hand, became so.[26]

Since it was potentially possible and desirable for every young lady to "become so," etiquette manuals flourished. In true democratic fashion, everyone who could afford one of these manuals and who could follow its advice theoretically had an equal opportunity to gain admittance into polite society. That and the right amount of money could make anyone, even a former milliner like Mrs. Tiffany, a "woman of fashion" as her husband calls her in the following excerpt from the play:

Tif.	And pray who made you a woman of fashion?
Mrs. Tif.	What a vulgar question! All the women of fashion, Mr. Tiffany —
Tif.	In this land are self-constituted, like you, Madam—and fashion is the cloak for more sins than charity ever covered! It was for fashion's sake that you insisted upon my purchasing this expensive house—it was for fashion's sake that you ran me in debt at every exorbitant upholsterer's and extravagant furniture warehouse in the city—it is for fashion's sake that you built that ruinous conservatory—hired more servants than they have persons to wait upon—and dressed your footman like a harlequin![27]

There was great tension in American society about these new "people of fashion," these constructors of new identities. People already entrenched in positions of prestige feared the dissipation of their authority and worried that access to money and a knowledge of certain forms were not sufficient indicators of fitness for the responsibilities that went along with social power. People who did not have the means to make the move upwards were envious and resentful that such distinctions still existed in a supposedly democratic society. Thus, rather than just being an American Mrs. Malaprop, Mrs. Tiffany, arguably the play's comic center, is the representation of the extreme social anxiety surrounding such "fashioned" people.

The theater itself was a denial of the democratic ideal. As can be seen from the description of the Park Theater given earlier, different classes of people were seated differently. Those in the cheapest and therefore least prestigious seats did have an equalizing way of making their voices heard. Sometimes called the "gallery gods" because of the power they wielded, those in the upper tiers made their displeasure known by hissing, stomping, or throwing refuse onto the stage and sometimes onto other viewers in more expensive seating. In *Letters of Jonathan Oldstyle*, Washington Irving relates the story of a time he was "saluted aside [his] head with a rotten pippen." When he rose to shake his cane at the gallery, he was restrained by a man behind him who warned him that this would bring down the full wrath of the people. The proper course of action, he was advised, was to "sit down quietly and bend your back to it."[28] Such incidents were an accepted method of releasing the tension created by hierarchical methods of segregating seating.

The upper and middle classes' new mania for fashion, however, only intensified the tension and hostility between the classes. The Astor Place Riot of 1848 was not, as some recent historians have pointed out, simply a result of the professional rivalry between the actors Macready and Forrest, but a demonstration by the lower classes against the ostentation of what they called the "codfish aristocracy." The Astor Place Opera House itself, as well as the dress and etiquette of its patrons, constituted an affront by a wealthy elite to traditional notions and republican simplicity in public.

The Astor Place Opera House (note that it was called an opera house not a theater) was built by members of New York's "upper ten" to replace the Park Theater. Most of the seating was reserved by subscription. Only five hundred seats were open to general admission in the gallery. To exclude prostitutes (and women of unlady-like independence), the house dictated that all ladies must be accompanied by a gentleman. There was also a dress code stipulating "freshly shaven faces, evening dress, fresh waistcoats, and kid gloves"—items not generally available to people of modest means. The rioters were not only demonstrating their preference for the emotional style of the vociferously American actor Forrest over the more restrained manner of the Englishman Macready, but also protesting the limiting of their access to entertainment through the exclusionary discipline of fashion.[29]

Although the play *Fashion* was written by an upper class person for the enjoyment and edification of others who belonged or aspired to the upper class, it also allowed for an expression of the hostility of people who had little or no hope of reaching positions of high social status. People who did not have a fashionable amount of French might not understand exactly why it was so funny that Mrs. Tiffany went around pronouncing all sorts of things "perfectly *recherche*," but any viewer could tell that all the characters putting on airs and pretending to be something they were not look like fools throughout the play and get their comeuppance at the end.

Fear and hostility also existed in those occupying the more expensive seats. To protect themselves against interlopers unfit for admission into the ranks of the respectable, makers of taste developed what writer Karen Halttunenn calls "the cult of sincerity."[30] People who are truly trustworthy, such a belief maintains, are sincere. Sincere people feel things deeply. They act and speak according to those beliefs. Adam Trueman, the model for male sincerity in the play, gives the following advice to Gertrude, the female ideal:

<blockquote>

Trueman: Never tell a lie, girl! not even for the sake of pleasing an old man! When you open your lips let your heart speak. Never tell a lie! Let your face be the looking-glass of your soul— your heart its clock—while your tongue rings the hours! But the glass must be clear, the clock true, and then there's no fear but the tongue will do its duty in a woman's head![31]

</blockquote>

Trueman, the play's true man, is a farmer who despite his wealth, still acts in a way that the more fashionable characters in the play describe as "rustic." He speaks his mind and acts boldly, becoming the single-handed savior for all the play's other troubled characters.

While the sentimentalists viewed men primarily as creatures of the mind who acted from reason, sincere women like Gertrude were creatures of the heart, acting largely from their affections. This greater sensitivity, or sensibility, gave women different responsibilities and liabilities from those of men. Sincere women functioned as measuring sticks by which sentimentalists gauged honest emotion. Sentimentalists felt that honest emotion was the ultimate indicator of worthiness in people and situations. They did not expect women to be logical thinkers or planners, but only to be able to distinguish between real and feigned emotion and to be in touch with the intuitive side of human knowledge. Therefore it is fitting that

Gertrude discover Jolimaitre to be an imposter. It does not matter so much that her impulsive plan to expose him backfires because of her own lack of forethought, but that she instinctively felt moved to take such an action. By the standards of the day, she was not being a stupid or weak character. She was only displaying her admirable innate sincerity.

Both these characters also display a Romantic preference for the natural over the constructed. Trueman, in contrast to the troubled dry-goods merchant, Mr.Tiffany, chose to make his living as a farmer and remain in unfashionable Catteraugus rather than fashionable New York. In the following excerpt, Trueman speaks of the misery of Tiffany, the self-made capitalist:

> You look as if you'd melted down your flesh into dollars, and mortgaged your soul in the bargain! Your warm heart has grown cold over your ledger—your light spirits heavy with calculation! You have traded away your youth—your hopes—your tastes for wealth! and now you have the wealth you coveted, what does it profit you? Pleasure it cannot buy; for you have lost your capacity for enjoyment—Ease it will not bring; for the love of gain is never satisfied! It has made your counting-house a penitentiary, and your home a fashionable museum where there is no niche for you! You have spent so much ciphering in the one, that you find yourself at last a very cipher in the other![32]

This passage, perhaps better than any other in the play, encapsulates the fears of Americans trying to make the transition from rural to urban living. Many felt, as Trueman expresses here, that they were trading a piece of their soul for material comfort.

Gertrude, forced by circumstance to live amongst the fashionable, implicitly delineates the differences between herself and social butterfly Seraphina Tiffany in the following ironically delivered speech:

> Can you suppose that I could possibly prefer a ramble in the woods to a promenade in Broadway? A wreath of scented wild flowers to a bouquet of these sickly exotics? The odor of new-mown hay to the heated air of this crowded conservatory? Or can you imagine that I could enjoy the quiet conversation of my Geneva friends more than the edifying chit-chat of a fashionable drawing room? But I see you think me totally destitute of taste![33]

Gertrude is rewarded with a husband at the end of the play, Seraphina is not.

Jolimaitre, the false French count (whose true European heritage is left ambiguous), represents the rampant fear of being duped that existed during that day. People were living in very big cities, in many cases for the first time. Unlike the small towns where these people came from, one could not expect to know the majority of people one encountered on the streets. It was necessary for these new urbanites to learn how to "read" or decipher nonverbal codes that would allow them to determine which individuals were worthy of their trust. If the city's sheer size and intricacy did not make it difficult enough for the uninitiated to make sense of its unreadable crowds, the elaborate deceptions perpetrated by many of its denizens made it impossible. Hosts of criminals set traps for the unwary. People and establishments of the most impeccable appearance could be completely untrustworthy. The story related earlier about Eldridge, the forger passing as a medical student in the house of a wealthy patron, is typical of the sorts of deceptions committed against the unwary.

John Kasson, in his book *Rudeness and Civility: Manners in Nineteenth-Century Urban America*, describes some even more frightening possibilities of deception. Some prostitutes and their procurers further added to their duplicity by being blackmailers. They contrived various ingenious traps to snare respectable men and women in compromising positions. As Kasson reports, an actual seduction was not always necessary. Anything that might lend itself to the appearance of scandal, no matter how innocent in fact, served their purposes equally well. For example, a businessman or even a minister might be naively led into a house of prostitution. Similarly, a "handsome and fashionably dressed street-lounger" might lure a respectable wife on a carriage ride, then sweep her away to a house or restaurant where he would attempt to ply her with "wine and wiles." Ultimately, whether his seduction was successful or not, the con man would threaten to inform the husband.[34]

The term "confidence man" itself originated at this time from the case of a single swindler who was finally caught in 1849. The man, Samuel Thompson, was a person of "genteel appearance" and remarkable audacity. He would approach a well-dressed stranger on the streets of a city and greet him as if he were an old acquaintance. After a brief conversation Thompson would ask, "Have you confidence in me to trust me with your watch until to-morrow?" The victim, too embarrassed to admit that he had forgotten the gentleman and reluctant to deny such a forthright request, would lend the watch. Then the "confidence man" walked off laughing, never to return.[35]

Fake nobles like "Count" Jolimaitre from the play were believed to be so common, many upper class people began to treat all foreigners, even those who appeared to be of their class, with a certain degree of suspicion. Englishwoman Isabella Bird, while visiting New York in 1856, wrote:

It must be stated that some of the most agreeable salons of New York are almost closed against foreigners. French, Germans, and Italians, with imposing titles, have proved how unworthily they bear them; and this feeling against strangers—I will not call it prejudice, for there are sufficient grounds for it—is extended to the English."[36]

Writers wrote books to educate novices about the depredations and horrors of the city. These authors issued grave warnings such as the following:

> [This volume] is designed to warn the thousands who visit the city against the dangers and pitfalls into which their curiosity or vice may lead them, and it is hoped that those who read the book will heed its warnings. The city is full of danger. The path of safety which is pointed out in these pages is the only one—a total avoidance of the vicinity of sin. No matter how clever a man may be in his own town or city, he is a child in the hands of the sharpers and villains of this community, and his only safety lies in avoiding them. His curiosity can be satisfied in these pages, and he can know the Great City from them, without incurring the danger attending an effort to see it.[37]

There would seem to be only three options open to those who did not wish to become victims of the many varieties of deception awaiting them in America's growing urban centers. One could either avoid the city altogether, as Adam Trueman does for the majority of his life; become a brilliant reader of the subtle clues that gave away the deceivers, like the prototype detectives in stories by Edgar Allan Poe; or follow the conservative guidelines set down by etiquette book writers to make oneself virtually invisible. In this last sense, fashion was not simply a style for displaying material abundance, but a guide to how wealthy or important people could protect themselves against those who might wish to prey on them.

Unlike the elaborately decorative dresses Mrs. Tiffany wears, the fashionable woman was advised to wear nothing on the public street that might draw attention to herself. Her respectability and physical safety might depend upon the signs she communicated through her appearance. Writing in 1837, Eliza Ware Farrar stressed: "singularity is to be avoided, and she is best dressed whose costume presents an agreeable whole, without anything that can be remarked."[38] Men's costumes also darkened steadily over the course of the century. A lady was encouraged to attend scrupulously to all aspects of her costume, avoiding overly rich materials, excessive displays of jewelry, heavy perfumes, and frayed or muddy skirt edges. Such details, etiquette writers warned, would be pitilessly examined, and her status as a true lady or vulgar pretender judged accordingly.[39]

On the street, sensible ladies or gentlemen strove to deport themselves in such a way that would offer nothing to arouse strangers' notice or give clues for a potential thief to seize upon. As Kasson states, through strict bodily control, each sought to create "a symbolic shield of privacy," which permitted one to move through a public space while "keeping aloof from engagement."[40]

Mowatt went to some length to let us know that the Tiffanys are breaking these rules. In addition to the showy ottomans, carpets, and conservatories to be seen on stage and discussed by the characters, each character's costumes were described by the author. Mrs. Tiffany appears in an "extravagant modern dress" with "hat, feathers, and mantle" in one act. Seraphina's costume was described as a "rich modern dress" with a "lady's tarpaulin on one side of her head." Even

Mrs. Tiffany's sister Prudence in addition to her old maid's costume of a black satin dress with a very narrow waist and tight sleeves, is sporting an old fashioned cap with a high top, broad frills and gaudy red ribbons.[41] All these have at least one feature guaranteed to draw the eye of an observer. All stand in stark contrast to Gertrude's more sensible house costume of a simple white muslin dress.

By dropping these details into the eyes and ears of those who could recognize and decipher them, Mowatt allowed the segment of her audience who knew and understood the rules of fashion to play a comforting game of "blame the victim." Villains and confidence men like Snobson and Jolimaitre are able to victimize the Tiffanys because of the greed of these aspirants to the upper-class and their lack of understanding of the rules of fashionable display. The ostentatious image they strive to project through their dress and possessions, rather than making them respectable, makes them visible and therefore vulnerable. Because Mrs. Tiffany knows only the forms of fashion without understanding the motivations and reasoning behind them, she invites the public gaze and therefore eventual disaster.

Audience members in the know could sit back and watch the Tiffanys fall victim to a sort of deception that they themselves feared somewhat in the manner that modern audiences watch teenage slasher films, saying to themselves, "That will never happen to me. I'm not that stupid." Although Poe complained about the contrived nature of the plot, I believe that it was this dramatization of deep-seated fears that made the play close enough to actual situations that members of the audience were trying to guess who the real Mrs. Tiffany was.

The unexpected success of *Fashion* was itself a testament to the growing awareness of and tolerance for theatricality as it was manifest in social life. Much of the comedy of the play depends on an ability to identify inappropriate tactics of self-promotion. Rather than condemning such deceptive behavior entirely, in the way a work from an earlier period of American history might have done, the play encourages audience members to look at such behavior in a milder and less judgmental light. The play's Tiffany family are not dangerous confidence men to be feared and shunned because of their desire to deceive, but are presented as comically inept bunglers in the gentle art of creating the illusion of being persons of high society. As Karen Halttunen points out, this attack on social theatricality, ironically was itself presented within a theatrical performance, and this critique of social ritual itself served as a ritual for its middle-class audiences. Many of the men and women who attended Mowatt's play went to laugh at the fashionable pretensions of their own class.[42]

The tensions and contradictions of attempting to act out the role of the honest and sincere citizen that the sentimentalists idolized without resorting to pretense had loosened enough by this time to enable audiences to laugh at the attempts of fictional others to establish and maintain a desirable social persona.

Another sign of the increased acceptance of the theatrical at this time was the growth in popularity of "parlor plays." Amateur productions had become quite common for middle-class Americans. Charades, pantomimes, readings and even full length plays were produced in private homes and community gathering places. Far from being recruiting grounds for the decadence of the stage and theatrical life, these productions were seen as innocent entertainment and wholesome education. Audiences of Anna Cora Mowatt's time were able to accept and dismiss her youthful explorations into theater, in part, because this activity was something that they were doing themselves in their own homes.[43] The acceptance of the theatrical in private was indicative of an increasingly sophisticated understanding of the use of guise in public life.

One dramatic form, the tableau, that has now faded in popularity was strikingly analogous to the sort of performance demanded daily of the respectable sentimentalist in the public realm. The stylized and controlled emotional self-expression demanded of parlor players in correctly executing tableaus was itself a caricature of the genteel performance demanded daily by sentimentalism. As in the tableau vivant, the true sentimentalist was expected to be able to strike the appropriate emotional expression and pose and to maintain them with flawless self-discipline under the eyes of his/her audience.[44] The theater, while still held in contempt as a profession, slowly gained recognition as a workable metaphor for social behavior.

More fear and hostility surface in the play's biting reference to politics. At one point, Adam Trueman exclaims:

Stop there! I object to your use of that word. When justice is found only among lawyers—health only among physicians—and patriotism among politicians, then may you say that there is no nobility where there are no titles![45]

Although people of the emerging American middle and upper classes were beginning to understand and accept the sort of theatricality that went on in the fashionable parlor or promenade, they did not necessarily like to see the same sort of things happening in the public arena. Like confidence men, a skillful politician could get what he wanted by playing the sincerity game.

This was a time during which the two party system came into the form we now recognize. One important characteristic of this new political age was the high degree of party organization which occurred to create mass support for a particular candidate. Although there was nothing new about the committee system, the intensity and range of committee organization to link the party to the largest number of people was unlike anything seen previously. General Andrew Jackson's election to the office of President was not so much the result of a popular groundswell as it was due to the political alterations that occurred at this time and the skill and determination of the new breed of politician who rallied in support of Jackson and constructed political apparatuses which would determine the electoral outcome. The great party leader, as Arthur Schlesinger says in his The Age of Jackson, was no longer the eloquent parliamentary orator, "whose fine periods could sweep his colleagues into supporting his measures, but the popular hero, capable of bidding directly for the confidences of the masses."[46]

Martin Van Buren, Jackson's vice president and eventually President of the United States himself, declared that true parliamentary leadership involved "powers of the mind more humble in pretension and less dazzling in appearance but, as experience has often proved, far more effective in the end than the most brilliant oratory when not sustained by them." Good judgment in timing measures, the capacity to strike directly at the opposition's weakest point without wasting time in "mere oratorical" disquisition, skill in guiding the debate so as to capitalize on "latent diversities of feeling and opinion on points either not at all or only remotely bearing upon the principal subject" and the good sense to strive for objects not beyond practical reach were more important techniques for the politician to master. Oratory, according to Van Buren, was useless without these technical skills and "the deep seated and habitual confidence" of a majority of the assembly and the people in general.[47]

Van Buren was typical of this new breed of politician. Despite his record of forceful leadership, Van Buren enjoyed a name for noncommittalism that survives when most other things about him have been forgotten. His nicknames - the

Little Magician, the American Tallyrand, the Red Fox of Kinderhook—suggest his popular reputation. Journalist Harriet Martineau wrote of him in 1838:

> There is much friendliness in his manners, for he is a kindhearted man: he is also rich in information, and lets it come out on subjects in which he cannot contrive to see any danger in speaking. But his manner wants the frankness and confidence which are essential to good breeding. He questions closely without giving anything in return. Moreover, he flatters to a degree which so cautious a man should long ago have found out to be disagreeable: and his flattery is not merely praise of the person he is speaking to, but a worse kind still,—a scepticism and ridicule of objects and persons supposed to be distasteful to the one he is conversing with. I fully believe that he is an amiable and indulgent domestic man, and a reasonable political master, a good scholar, and a shrewd man of business: but he has the scepticism which marks the low orders of politicians. His public career exhibits no one exercise of that faith in men, and preference of principle to petty expediency by which a statesman show himself to be great.[48]

John Quincy Adams, who lost his re-election bid to Jackson, expressed the baffled exasperation of the old school in an outburst against James K. Polk, who eventually became president after Van Buren: "He has no wit, no literature, no point of argument, no gracefulness of delivery, no elegance of language, no philosophy, no pathos, no felicitous impromptus; nothing that can constitute an orator, but confidence, fluency and labor."[49]

It was therefore probably with great feeling that Anna Cora Mowatt, friend of Adams' vice president and great orator Henry Clay, had *Fashion*'s arch-deceiver Count Jolimaitre mock the futility of Gertrude's protestations at the moment he believes her in his clutches by saying, "My charming little orator, patriotism and declamation become you particularly!"[50]

With the increased awareness of private social interaction as theatrical came the knowledge that public interaction, specifically politics, was also a big confidence game that could be played badly or well. Politicians were becoming successful by following the same rules of simplicity and sincerity that fashion set down for cautious members of the upper class. These men, like discreet gentlewomen on the street, had to be aware of and bow to public gaze and opinion. Ralph Waldo Emerson wrote the following about American politics of that period:

> In dealing with the State we ought to remember that its institutions are not aboriginal, though they existed before we were born, that they are not superior to the citizen; that every one of them was once the act of a single man; every law and usage was a man's expedient to meet a particular case; that they are all imitable, all alterable; we may make as good, we may make better. Society is an illusion to the young citizen. It lies before him in rigid repose, with certain names, men and institutions rooted like oak-trees to the center, round which all arrange themselves the best they can. But the old statesman knows that society is fluid; there are no such roots and centers, but any particle may suddenly become the center of the movement and compel the system to gyrate around it... (O)ur institutions, though in coincidence with the spirit of the age, have not any exemption from the practical defects which have discredited other forms.

> Every actual State is corrupt. Good men must not
> obey the laws too well. What satire on government
> can equal the censure of the word politic, which now
> for ages has signified cunning, intimating that the
> state is a trick?[51]

These were frightening times for people interested in maintaining a stable base of power and the status quo. Political and social change was rampant. Labor leaders such as George Henry Evans, Thomas Skidmore, Seth Luther, and Ely Moore tried to stir the conscience of the nation about the problems of urban workers. Dorothea L. Dix spent her life working to win improvements in mental institutions. Other activists worked for prison reform. In 1848, the first convention for equal rights for women was held in Seneca Falls, New York. Frances Wright, Lucretia Mott, Susan B. Anthony, and Elizabeth Cady Stanton were among the early leaders of this movement. The American Temperance Union formed in Boston in 1826. New England Transcendentalists organized the Brook Farm in West Roxbury, Massachusetts, in 1841. John Humphrey Noyes founded the Oneida Community in 1848 in Seneca Falls, New York. William Miller of New York predicted the Second Coming of Christ on October 22, 1844. Millerites, despite the fact that the promised apocalypse did not occur, evolved into the Seventh-day Adventist Church. In the 1830's, Joseph Smith published *The Book of Mormon*. Followers of Smith led by Brigham Young founded the Mormon community in Salt Lake City, Utah, in 1848.

Americans everywhere were attempting to adopt new patterns of life. They joined voluntary associations in droves to eliminate crippling social disabilities and restructure their society. Philip Hone, writing in 1840, characterized this aggressive outlook as the "go ahead" attitude. "We have become the most careless, reckless, headlong people on the face of the earth," he complained. "'Go ahead' is our maxim and password; and we do go ahead with a vengeance, regardless of consequences and indifferent about the value of human life."[52] In *Fashion*, Adam Trueman displays a similar attitude when he cautions the capitalist Tiffany:

> I hear you are making money on the true, American, high pressure system—better go slow and sure—the more steam, the greater danger of the boiler's bursting![53]

Another writer named John L. O'Sullivan, editor of *The Democratic Review*, wrote an essay in 1845 that coined an even more popular term for the prevalent American mental disposition. In discussing the American claim to the new territory in the west, he stated:

> (It) is by the right of our manifest destiny to overspread and to possess the whole of the continent which Providence has given us for the development of the great experiment of liberty and the federative self-government entrusted to us. It is a right such as that of the tree to the space of air and earth suitable for the full expansion of its principle and destiny of growth.[54]

Manifest Destiny signified a glowing faith in democracy and a passionate desire that it rule the world. Unfortunately, it also served as a mask for speculation in land and Texas scrip and a rationalization for the brutal removal of Native Americans from their homes in the Eastern seaboard and the provocation of the Mexican American War in 1846. However, manifest destiny did express an honest idealism in Americans about the future of the world. The only group of people who did not share this optimism were on the political right.

Democratic congressman Robert Rantoul charged in 1848 that conservative enmity to expansion was part of their old scheme to keep wages down:

> So long as cheap land continues to be abundant, so long as you cannot drive the wages of labor to the starvation point... Here, then, is the way in which a comprehensive democratic statesmanship would begin to protect labor: by affording it ample room, scope sufficient to work out its will upon the whole unoccupied North American continent.[55]

Whether or not this charge was accurate, the established, moneyed class of Americans did find themselves in the uncomfortable position of being caught up in a popular spirit of expansionism and experimentation under the leadership of men they did not feel they could trust. Many who may have been privately fuming or shaking in their boots were quick to rattle their canes in agreement with Adam Trueman when he proclaimed:

> This fashion-worship has made heathens and hypocrites of you all! Deception is your household God! A man laughs as if he were crying, and cries as if he were laughing up his sleeve. Everything is something else from what it seems to be. I have lived in your house only three days, and I've heard more lies than were ever invented during a Presidential election![56]

Despite the popular mood of liberalism, Anna Cora Mowatt did not hurt herself by writing a play with such strong conservative undercurrents. To begin with, she had to display a deep knowledge of her subject in order to induce her audience even to listen to her play. As the acerbic comments of the drama correspondent for *Spirit of the Times* and Epes Sargent's prologue to *Fashion* point out, Mowatt had several extratextual obstacles to overcome before she could gain a fair hearing for her work from her audience. Being a woman, an American, and a first-time author were three marks against her before she began. In the following excerpt from *The Narrative Act*, Susan Lanser discusses the difficulty of establishing narrative authority:

Communicators can also affect the status of their message, and of themselves as writers, through the skill they demonstrate in performing the speech act. A vividly told, detailed narrative by a writer of little status might produce a degree of stature for the text which far exceeds that originally bestowed on the writer. This experience has been common, if fact, for the woman writer, of whom so little has been expected that she has sometimes been treated as a curiosity—as Johnson's "dog walking on its hind legs"—or is presumed to have achieved the illusion of skill spontaneously, as if by accident.[57]

Therefore the authority of Mowatt's text had to come from her audience's recognition of her skillful construction of the tale rather than from their respect for her as a person. Display of what Poe disparagingly dismissed as the "very carpets, the very ottomans, the very chandeliers, and the very conservatories" of the fashionable set were an important part of Mowatt's bid for credibility. Not only did she reveal her insider's knowledge of what was "in" and "out" with the well-heeled, her careful contrasting of the foolishly ostentatious Tiffanys with sincere Truemans showed Mowatt's mastery of her subject.

As Poe pointed out, Mowatt did not simply ridicule fashionable follies, or the things that an outsider would find ridiculous. Her comedy cut to the heart of upper class discomfort with the artificiality and accessibility of fashion as a royal road to social power. In *Fashion*, Mowatt pointed out that fashion sometimes leads people to do things that look foolish to the uninitiated and that the ignorant following of the forms of fashion can lead people do to things that are foolish and dangerous. Mowatt's writing shows that she knew not only the right ottomans, carpets, and conservatories, but why an established member of the upper class would believe it was dangerous for people like the Tiffanys to have them.

Through the words of characters whose actions are rewarded in the play, Mowatt reified the political conservatism and reactionary attitudes of her upper class auditors. Since the outlook of her intended audience was conservative, the skillful display of such leanings by valorized characters in *Fashion* only enhanced her narrative authority.

Among liberals as well as conservatives, lower class people as well as the upper class, the aggressive optimism of the American public of the mid-1840's was coupled with reservations about the implications of the rapid changes taking place in their society. Although Mowatt's philosophical alignment with upper class conservatism might have been hard for a general audience of mixed views to stomach as a tragedy, as a comedy it was palatable because it offered the opportunity to vent feelings of hostility and fear. Because the characters and situations were so exaggerated, the audience was free to use them as straw men representing a number of disagreeable tendencies in their society. To one audience member, Mrs. Tiffany might be a ridiculous representative of the hated "codfish aristocracy." To another, she could be a laughable bungler of the rules of genteel society. A liberal auditor might nod in agreement with Adam Trueman's condemnation of the pretensions of the fashionable set. A conservative could rattle his cane in affinity with Trueman's subtle salvos at radical egalitarianism. Despite the fear and hostility that divided them, an American audience of the 1840's could laugh together at *Fashion*, each believing him/herself clever enough to avoid the pitfalls the Tiffanys—the very characters who make the play uniquely American—are too foolish to avoid.

By accurately tapping into a myriad of nagging fears and anxieties in her audience about the growing artificiality of interaction in urban life, Anna Cora Mowatt was able to craft a play that appealed to a broad spectrum of viewers. This deft demonstration of her mimetic abilities in turn created a self as the implied author that was worthy of her auditors' attention and admiration. Thus through skillful and timely storytelling, Anna Cora Mowatt, a novice female American playwright, won from a grudging potential audience the right to a public voice.

CHAPTER 6

EXPLOITING THE MEDIUM:
ANNA CORA MOWATT'S CREATION OF SELF
THROUGH PERFORMANCE

In this chapter, I wish to look at the way Anna Cora Mowatt created a self through performance. However, rather than focus on records of her public performances, I wish to examine the existing accounts of a dramatic creation of Mowatt's that only a few of her closest friends were privileged to see. In this private theatrical, the tensions inherent in Mowatt's public self show through.

In October of 1841, Anna Cora Mowatt embarked on a critically and popularly successful career as a public reader. By the winter of 1843, however, she had to cancel all engagements abruptly because of a severe respiratory illness. She was an invalid for the better part of the next four years. In hopes of relieving this condition, she began a series of treatments from Dr. William Francis Channing in what at that time was called "mesmerism." The treatment yielded some remarkable results.

Mowatt devoted an entire chapter of her autobiography to a description of the unusual cure she underwent. Her friend Epes Sargent echoed her account in his book *The Scientific Basis of Spiritualism* published in 1881. According to Mowatt and Sargent, mesmerism not only relieved Anna Cora's respiratory distress but elevated her to a higher state of consciousness where she could do all sorts of incredible things. She could write perfect letters and embroider beautifully in absolute darkness, predict crises in her illness to the exact day and hour, diagnose illness in others and remain insensible to pain. She reportedly sat through the extraction of one of her molars by a dentist without anesthesia. At times she seemed to be telepathic. Mowatt, under mesmeric influence, developed a second personality who called herself the "Gypsy" and Mowatt's waking self the "little Fool." The Gypsy wrote many poems and stories and loved to debate philosophy and religion for hours with Sargent and her husband, James Mowatt.

Sargent and the Mowatts were not the only people experimenting with mesmerism at this time. Mesmerism was one of the many "ism's" that surfaced and attracted followings during the nineteenth century. Transcendentalism, communitarianism, spiritualism, and Adventism and many other popular movements were also sweeping the country and gaining converts. As Robert C. Fuller stated in *Mesmerism and the American Cure of Souls*, each of these movements expressed popular dissatisfactions while simultaneously creating vehicles for both personal and social innovations.[1] The influence of these "ism" movements in America did not end with the turn of the century. Fuller saw mesmerism as one of the first of many attempts to supply unchurched Americans with a spiritual philosophy of life. He called the movement, "America's first non-ecclesiastical practice of spiritual healing."[2] Mesmerism, along with Spiritualism, is the parent of the currently popular New Age beliefs. Many tenets and manifestations of New Age religions appear in original form in Spiritualist texts and the writings of mesmerists and their clients.

Mesmerism, unlike other "ism" movements, was not a sect, experimental social program, or a distinctive theological creed. Mesmerism got its name from Anton Mesmer, a physician who in the mid-eighteenth century began experimenting with treatments for nervous disorders. He postulated that there was an invisible, impalpable fluid that permeated the entire universe and emanated from the stars, the sun, the planets, the earth, and from human bodies as well. To distinguish it from ferromagnetism, Mesmer had called the invisible fluid *magnetisme animal.* "Animal," in this case, was used to mean vital.

Mesmer's treatment was different from what we today call hypnotism. Induced somnambulism actually originated with the Marquis de Puysegur in 1784. The Marquis, a student of Mesmer's, appropriated his teacher's terminology to describe his new technique.[3]

Charles Poyen, a young Frenchman, first popularized animal magnetism in the United States through a series of lectures in Boston on the subject early in 1836. Dr. Joseph du Commun, an instructor in French at West Point, had also delivered a series of three lectures on animal magnetism during the summer of 1829 in Fanny Wright's famous Hall of Science in New York.

Pamphleteers and tract writers generated innumerable short works promoting or decrying mesmerism. *The Philosophy of Animal Magnetism: Together with the System of Manipulating Adopted to Produce Ecstasy and Somnambulism—The Effects and the Rationale*, written by an author identifying himself only as "A Gentleman of Philadelphia" and published in 1937 by Philadelphian printers Merrihew and Gunn, is typical of the sort of inexpensive publications that were available to inform curious readers about the powers of mesmerism. The author begins his text with a description of the sensation created by the mesmerists:

> Animal Magnetism, owing to recent developments of extraordinary facts, the attestation of which are too well sustained to be refuted, begins powerfully to engage the attention of all classes of

society in our country. These facts, spread before the community, without the least pretence on the part of our fellow citizens to understand anything of the cause, have startled and surprised them. They have burst suddenly upon them, like a flood of light pouring its beams into a dungeon, almost before they were prepared to suspect their existence; for, unless to the learned, even its name was hardly known until recently to ordinary readers, and its meaning still fewer pretended to understand. At the apparitional presence of a power so stupendous, our alarm has prevented that calm investigation demanded by phenomena so remote from the ordinary course of events.[4]

The author himself was not able to keep his investigation calm for very long and was soon denouncing mesmerism's foes and exalting its virtues in a kinetic combination of typefaces.

Animal magnetism, until now, seems to have been chiefly understood in its results and effects, and many things connected with it have been entirely above our philosophy. In consequence of this, it came in conflict with the pride of learning, because it did not open a sufficiently wide field for *speculation*. The literati could not revel in conjecture, and perhaps one of the reasons why it has not been acceptable to many is, that it has to do with a science which PROVES THE EXISTENCE OF A SOUL IN MAN; being the *connecting link* between *physiology* and *psychology*, the former confining its labors to the physical machines, and the latter considering man as a compound of body and spirit. Investigations, however, prove animal magnetism to have a more especial connection with psychology, than with any other doctrine or science.[5]

More than establishing a link between psychology and physiology, the author was concerned with establishing mesmerism as justification for traditional Christian beliefs in the face of emerging scientific theories about the nature and functioning of the human brain.

Mesmerism, he explained at one point, is a scientific application of the non-scientific concept faith.

The demonstrations of animal magnetism are *practical* faith; that is, the operator must be able to confine his thoughts to one point, and fix them there. No man can exercise what is called faith, who is not able to do this, it being an essential prerequisite. To doubt, then, is to lose faith, for it is to distract. When the mind wanders from the point upon which it is fixed, it can no longer exercise this conservative principle. Thus it was when Christ walked on the water.[6]

Because mesmerism could be observed under what were considered scientific conditions and still not be completely explained away by rational means, the phenomenon was for the author proof that science did not hold all the answers to life's questions. "Animal magnetism," he concluded, "is a powerful support of true religion, and the more it is known, so much more will Christianity be unshackled of its embarrassments and appear divested of its dross."[7]

Mesmerism even worked its way into literature of the time. Both Balzac and Dumas used mesmerism as a plot device in novels written during the first half of the nineteenth century. In *The Blithedale Romance* (first published in 1852), American author Nathaniel Hawthorne assumed a readership at least partially familiar with mesmerism and the phenomena alleged to occur to subjects in mesmeric trances. A subplot of the novel involves a mesmerist who schemes to use his powers to gain control over an unsuspecting young woman. "Human will was but soft wax in his hands," the narrator says of the evil mesmerist.[8]   He described this unsettling character in the following passage:

> I heard, from a pale man in blue spectacles, some stranger stories than were written in a romance; told, too, with a simple, unimaginative steadfastness, which was terribly efficacious in compelling the auditor to receive them into the category of established facts. He cited instances of the miraculous power of one human being over the will and passions of another; insomuch that settled grief was but a shadow, beneath the influence of a man possessing this potency, and the strong love of years melted away like a vapor. At the bidding of one of these wizards, the maiden, with her lover's kiss still burning on her lips, would turn from him with icy indifference; the newly made widow would dig up her buried heart out of her young husband's grave, before the sods had taken root upon it; a mother, with her babe's milk in her bosom, would thrust away her child.[9]

A few pages later, Hawthorne gave us a glimpse of an exhibition by the mesmerist that was probably very like ones that Hawthorne himself may have seen.

> The Professor began his discourse, explanatory of the psychological phenomena, as he termed them, which it was his purpose to exhibit to the spectators. There remains no very distinct impression of it on my memory. It was eloquent, ingenious, plausible, with a delusive show of spirituality, yet really imbued throughout with a cold and dead materialism.   I shivered, as a current of chill air, issuing out of a

sepulchral vault and bringing the smell of corruption along with it. He spoke of a new era that was dawning upon the world; an era that would link soul to soul, and the present life to what we call futurity, with a closeness that should finally convert both worlds into one great, mutually conscious brotherhood. He described (in a strange, philosophical guise, with terms of art, as if it were a matter of chemical discovery) the agency by which this mighty result was to be effected; nor would it have surprised me, had he pretended to hold up a portion of his universally pervasive fluid, as he affirmed it to be, in a glass phial.

At the close of his exordium, the Professor beckoned with his hand - once, twice, thrice - and a figure came gliding upon the platform, enveloped in a long veil of silvery whiteness. It fell about her, like the texture of a summer cloud, with a kind of vagueness, so that the outline of the form, beneath it, could not be accurately discerned. But the movement of the Veiled Lady was graceful, free, and unembarrassed, like that of a person accustomed to be the spectacle of thousands. Or, possibly, a blindfolded prisoner within the sphere with which this dark, earthly magician had surrounded her, she was unconscious of being the central object to all those straining eyes.[10]

In this work, pre-dating George Du Maurier's *Trilby* (published in 1894) by several decades, Hawthorne exploits the horrific potential of a Svengali-like character to take control of another's soul through the exercise of a superior will and the medium of mesmerism.

Edgar Allan Poe was also well acquainted with mesmerism. He witnessed several subjects being placed into "magnetic trances" and even attended a mesmeric séance performed by renowned spiritualist Andrew Jackson Davis. In an article entitled "Mesmeric Revelation" that originally appeared in *Columbian Lady's and Gentleman's Magazine* in August of 1844, Poe recorded a session in which he mesmerized a Mr. Vankirk and questioned him about various spiritual matters. "Whatever doubt may still envelop the rationale of mesmerism," Poe insisted in the article, "its startling facts are now almost universally admitted."[11] He went on to describe to skeptics what he believed to be the laws of mesmerism and its general features:

> There can be no more absolute waste of time than the attempt to prove, at the present day, that man, by the mere exercise of will, can so impress his fellow as to cast him into an abnormal condition, of which the phenomena resemble very closely those of death, or at least resemble them more nearly than they do the phenomena of any other normal condition within our cognizance; that, while in this state, the person so impressed employs only with effort, and then feebly, the external organs of sense, yet perceives, with keenly refined perception, and through channels supposed unknown, matters beyond the scope of the physical organs; that moreover, his intellectual faculties are wonderfully exalted and invigorated; that his sympathies with the person so impressing him are profound; and finally, that his susceptibility to the impression increases with its frequency, while in the same proportion, the peculiar phenomena elicited are more extended and more pronounced.[12]

Poe made more sensational use of his knowledge of mesmerism in his short story "The Facts of the Case of M. Valdemar," originally printed in the December, 1845, issue of

American Review. M. Valdemar, knowing he is dying, requests the narrator to put him into a mesmeric trance. Valdemar hopes to obtain immortal life in this manner, but instead finds his consciousness trapped gruesomely in a lifeless body until the mesmerist releases him to a natural death.

The story was reprinted in London in 1846 as a three pence pamphlet entitled *Mesmerism "in Articulo Mortis;" An Astounding and Horrifying Narrative Showing the Extraordinary Power of Mesmerism in Arresting the Progress of Death*. Readers took the work in this form as fact rather than fiction and were scandalized by its implications.

In addition to the novelty of the topic, in those days before the development of reliable anesthetics there was a good deal of medical interest in mesmerism because of its reported ability to render a subject insensible to pain. As their choice of terminology indicates, these researchers considered the mesmerized subject to be put into a special state resembling sleep. In 1823, Dr. A. Bertrand of the respected Nancy school devoted to the study of the subject listed the distinguishing characteristics of what he called "artificial somnambulism":

1. Spontaneous post-somnambulic amnesia
2. Spontaneous analgesia
3. Acute sense of timing
4. Hallucinatory activity
5. Improved ability to recall
6. Thought transmission
7. Sight without eyes
8. Control of own physiological processes
9. Ability to prescribe remedies for various illness
10. Prophesy with regard to future course of illness
11. Mental inertia (hypersuggestibilty, compliance, and inability to initiate acts)
12. Ability to take on the illness of another person, thereby curing the latter.[13]

Today, experts in the field of hypnotism reject many of these characteristics as accurate descriptions of the phenomenon we now call hypnosis. The term hypnosis itself has fallen into disfavor with researchers because of its erroneous linkage of the phenomenon to sleep. The orientation of research into hypnotic phenomena over the past half century has turned instead to a number of theories of hypnosis which can loosely be called "social psychological" in orientation.[14] This approach differs from more traditional concepts of hypnosis because it rejects the utility of terms such as "hypnotic state," "trance," "altered state of consciousness" and "waking state." The social psychological approach instead stresses terms such as attitudes, beliefs, expectations, conformity, compliance, imagination, and relaxation. Proponents of the social psychological perspective see hypnosis not as some kind of physiological state that is transmitted genetically, but as a social invention which is transmitted culturally.

Most hypnotic situations are social situations in which hypnotist and subject act out roles. As Graham F. Wagstaff stated in his article, "Suggestibility: A Social Psychological Approach," the role of the subject is to present himself or herself as "hypnotized" according to previous expectations and cues given indirectly or directly by the hypnotist and the immediate context.[15] Although this approach does not assume that all hypnotic subjects are actively "faking" (though they may be), it does assume that the subject will try very hard to enact the hypnotic role and may attempt to use a variety of techniques or strategies to bring about various effects. Wagstaff cites the example of a subject who, when it is suggested that his/her arms are heavy, may try very hard to make his/her arms heavy by imaginatively participating with the suggestion. When a hypnotist suggests that the subject will feel no pain, a cooperative subject may try distraction, or imagining a pleasant scene. Research that indicates the very best hypnotic subjects have personalities that can be characterized as "fantasy prone" supports this conjecture.[16] In other words, the best subjects are those who are the most adept at pretending.

Today, none of these fantastic claims may seem credible to a modern reader. What, then, actually happened? Were Mowatt and Sargent lying or perpetuating a con? Did the phenomenon called mesmerism lose some of its potency when its name changed to hypnosis?

Neither Mowatt nor Sargent would seem to have the usual motivations for perpetrating a fraud. Both were living in states of relative affluence at this time. They were near neighbors in fashionable New York apartments. Neither made any money directly from the experience. Mrs. Mowatt did not, like some other virtuoso mesmeric subjects, consent to let herself be exhibited publicly for researchers and the curious. Although the mention of Mrs. Mowatt's fantastic experience with mesmerism may have contributed to the sale of both Mowatt's and Sargent's books, neither book focuses exclusively or even primarily on her mesmeric experiences.

Why then did they make the claims they did? Were they delusional? Were they reporting things they wanted to see? Were they stretching the truth to make their lives seem more interesting and their experience unique? The answer that I put forth here is that neither Mowatt nor Sargent was actively perpetrating a cynical fraud to deceive the credulous. They were performing. Anna Cora Mowatt and her good friend Epes Sargent were performing in a social drama of such intensity that their upper-class Victorian minds would not let them openly admit the name of their play or claim the roles they were playing. The character of the "Gypsy" Mowatt created under mesmerism was no less false or performed than roles she played in real life.

If we can therefore assume that the fantastic abilities with which Anna Cora Mowatt was reportedly gifted while under the influence of mesmerism were not the results of being elevated to a supernatural state, how can we explain them in terms of role-playing? From the facts about her life, Mowatt seems to fit the typical profile of an ideal hypnotic subject. Her numerous works of fiction attest to her imaginative nature. She was adept enough at pretending to become a highly acclaimed stage actress. Edgar Allan Poe described her on stage:

> In the utterance of the truly generous, of the really noble, of the unaffectedly passionate, we see her bosom heave, her cheek grow pale, her limbs tremble, her lip quiver, and nature's own tear rush impetuously to the eye. She looks, speaks, and moves with a well-controlled impulsiveness, as different as can be conceived from the customary rant and cant, the hack conventionality of the stage.[17]

Although there is no way of knowing how her acting style would contrast to modern actors, all Mowatt's critics agreed that her greatest strength as a performer was the unaffected ease with which she played her roles. The same skills that allowed her to charm the public in Park Theater could have also convinced a much smaller drawing room audience that they were speaking with a personality completely different from the Anna Cora they knew.

Advocates of the social psychological approach to hypnotic phenomena also stress the existence of a cooperative relationship between subject and hypnotist. From Epes Sargent's accounts, Mowatt was extremely attuned to the moods of her mesmerizer. He claimed that if he put anything hot or cold into his mouth, she would at once recognize it. Unless, he hastened to add significantly, her attention was directed to something else at the moment.[18] Although Mowatt's and Sargent's accounts make it clear that Dr. Channing, who is named only as Dr. C——g by Mowatt, was in charge of the mesmeric treatment for her respiratory illness, Sargent indicates that he mesmerized her almost daily over the period. He claimed that he needed only to wave his hand over her a few times to induce the trance-state in her. As he describes the process:

> By a few passes of my hand without contact I could throw her into what seemed a profound state of coma, rarely lasting more than a minute, from which she would emerge in a state of consciousness, which, though it commanded all the contents of her normal state, was evidently distinct and superior. Her eyeballs were rolled up and the lids drooped loosely, though when she became animated in conversation the lids would close tightly, and her countenance became more expressive than the open eye could have made it.[19]

Mowatt was accustomed to submissively accepting the guidance of older men. She adored her father and continued to consult him on all her major life decisions until his death. James Mowatt, a lawyer thirteen years her senior, convinced her to elope with him when she was fifteen. He directed all her subsequent education, hiring tutors for her in various subjects and creating extensive reading lists for her in all his favorite topics. Sargent was also an important advisor to Mowatt. Every important step she took as a creative artist was made with his advice and support. Poe marked the similarities between Sargent's popular play *Velasco* and Mowatt's phenomenally successful melodrama *Fashion*. He accounted for the similarity by saying:

> "Velasco," compared with American tragedies generally, is a good tragedy—indeed an excellent one, but, positively considered, its merits are very

inconsiderable. It has many of the traits of Mrs. Mowatt's "Fashion" to which, in its mode of construction, its scenic effects, and several other points, it bears as close a resemblance, as, in the nature of things, it could very well bear. It is by no means improbable, however, that Mrs. Mowatt received some assistance from Mr. Sargent in the composition of her comedy, or at least was guided by his advice in many particulars of technicality.[20]

Poe did not seem to have entertained the reverse notion that Mowatt could have aided Sargent in the composition of his plays. Mowatt herself in a letter to Sargent's brother said that the play was originally written to amuse Sargent and her husband.

Mowatt was not simply a willing slave, though. Sargent repeatedly remarks on her independence:

There was a quick sympathy with all my moods and physical conditions, and yet she was supremely and independently conscious all the time, and would reason upon the phenomena, describe them, philosophize upon them, and oppose my own opinions with an ability far transcending that which she exhibited in her normal state.[21]

Her official hypnotist was also charmed by this same characteristic:

Channing was much pleased and interested, for he found her giving back to him, in many instances, his own thoughts; but at the same time maintaining independent views on some points. That she was in a state quite distinct from her normal state he was fully satisfied. Her earnest but childlike manner, the tone of her voice, the character of her thoughts, her eyes with the lids hanging loose and the balls rolled up, were all peculiarities that did not fail to impress him.[22]

At times, Sargent reported, Mowatt in her "higher state" even assumed the roles of the authority figures themselves:

> She, in her abnormal state, was always her own physician, and her own despotic ruler, showing absolute confidence in all her prescriptions. Still she seemed acutely sensitive to the mesmerizer's unexpressed will, especially in her normal state. While somnambulic she wished me to give her the power of passing from her abnormal to her normal state, and to effect this, she directed me to magnetize her ring, so that in my absence she could, by pulling it off, pass into her usual condition.[23]

In addition to exhibiting all the behaviors her mesmerizers expected to see and probably unconsciously guided her to perform, Mowatt retained a mind and will of her own. Rather than convincing her mesmerizers that their efforts were incompletely successful, this lack of complete cooperation seemed to make the experience more exciting, more authentic for them. The perfect hypnotic subject for them was one who was submissive enough to go along with the game but independent enough to maintain their interest and make the imposition of their will onto another's seem a challenge.

Although Sargent spoke of inducing the trance state "without contact" in one of the passages quoted above, mesmerism did involve a good deal of casual contact between subject and hypnotist. Indeed, Mowatt was very particular about contact with her in her higher state:

> She would be agitated by the touch of any one except her husband or her mesmerizer, unless the person touching her was previously put *en rapport* with her, or "in communication," as she termed it, by the mesmerizer.[24]

Mowatt was a young, very attractive, upper class, married Victorian lady with a sick, older husband. As Sargent said, James Mowatt "took an intelligent interest in the phenomena"; however the lawyer's state of health did not allow him to "exert the mesmeric influence himself."[25] The whole affair was innocent enough that both Mowatt and Sargent published public accounts of it, yet questionable enough that Mowatt chose to conceal the identity of her mesmerists. Sargent always carefully mentioned the presence of her husband during mesmeric experiences.

It is possible that mesmerism was an expression of an unacknowledged sexual attraction between the two of them. They were close, life-long friends. They shared many interests, somewhat more than either seemed to share with James Mowatt. Anna Cora was a famous beauty of her day. Contemporary Edgar Allan Poe gave the following description of Epes Sargent dating from around the time he was mesmerizing Mrs. Mowatt:

> In a word, he is one of the most prominent members of a very extensive American family—the men of industry, talent, and tact. In stature he is short—not more than five feet five—but well proportioned. His face is a fine one; the features regular and expressive. His demeanor is very gentlemanly. Unmarried, and about thirty years of age.[26]

There is no evidence that their relationship ever took any other form of expression. However, the evidence of both accounts strongly suggests that Anna Cora Mowatt performed her most fantastic somnambulic feats out of a subconscious desire to please Epes Sargent. Under hypnosis, she created an ideal woman for him—intellectual, spiritual, imaginative, fearless, and independent or as Sargent himself describes her:

> In her abnormal state there was that perfect self-poise, intelligence, and self-control which made the idea of a merely morbid development ridiculous. She seemed to look down upon all the contents of her normal memory as from a superior position. In Mrs. Mowatt's case, the state was in every respect a superior one, intellectually, morally and, I may add, physically...[27]

Sargent's book makes it clear that he had a good deal invested in the phenomena of Mesmerism—not financially, but intellectually. For him, it was more than merely a particularly exciting parlor game. He was a man looking for answers. Like many educated people of his day he was uncomfortable with and became increasingly more concerned about the replacement of faith with science in his age. In reaction, he turned to Spiritualism, which was for him the investigation of phenomena unexplainable by science. Thus he became one of the many involved in what one writer called "the quest for a peculiarly nineteenth-century Grail," the positive and intellectually acceptable proof of immortality cleared of any association with fraud or humbug.[28] In his book, tellingly titled *The Scientific Basis of Spiritualism*, Sargent asserted:

The convictions of seers, mediums, and intuitionalists generally, in favor of a spiritual organism involving the universal presence of the mind in the physical body, may be fairly accepted as confirming the philosophical views of Ulrici, Walter, Hoffman, and others on this particular subject and are an earnest [affirmation] that Cartesian dogma has had its day, and must soon give way to the re-establishment of the old Pauline doctrine, as affirmed by Spiritualism. Thus does the most advanced philosophical analysis come to the support of the great generalization from our facts, that there is in man a psychical organism, released from the physical by death, and carrying the guaranty not only of his continuous life, but of his unimpaired individuality in all its essentials.[29]

Therefore Sargent was highly motivated to see and report manifestations of powers beyond explanation. His witnessing of Mowatt's remarkable abilities under hypnosis was contact with a higher state of mankind that he felt sure could not be explained by scientists like Darwin who would seem to level man with animal.

Anna Cora Mowatt is also likely to have had ulterior motivations for going along with the mesmeric experiment. Her primary stated reason for allowing herself to be mesmerized was to improve her health. She found great satisfaction in this treatment as she stated in the following letter to Helen Whitman:

> I believe you have heard that I owe my restoration almost entirely to magnetic influence? That great and heaven-blessed power, which placed in the hands of a high-minded, feeling and scientific man, is capable of applying balm to one half the mental and bodily ills of suffering humanity. The subject must be one of great interest to you who have yourself been a magnetizer, but think what a charm it must possess for me, I who have had a thousand pains soothed, a thousand annoyances (not to say griefs) banished, vigor restored to every limb, almost life

itself given back, and a holy calm shed over my whole existence through its happy medium.[30]

It is clear that Mowatt found relief from her suffering through mesmerism. What is less clear is the nature of her illness. Contemporaries and biographers have identified the condition variously as respiratory fatigue, acute bronchitis, and mild tuberculosis. Epes Sargent called it a "congestion of the brain."[31] James Mowatt told Mary Howitt several years later that his wife's physicians "gave it as their opinion that the shock which her feelings had sustained and not her physical and mental exertions, was killing her."[32]

Several of Mowatt's friends and family had reacted badly to her decision to become a public reader. In particular, Mowatt later told a nephew that she was upset by an aunt who had been very close who completely cut off communication. Not only did her experiment with mesmerism afford her the chance to be treated like someone special, it also turned a psychosomatic response to stress and anxiety into a legitimate illness that could be treated by persons she deemed "high-minded and moral men of science." If friends and family had rejected her as a pariah for overstepping the bounds of class propriety by going on the stage, mesmerism gave her caring treatment from authority figures who she trusted and respected. Mesmerism indeed served as a happy medium, passing her from depression and suffering back to self-confidence and optimism.

Like Sargent, Mowatt also found spiritual answers in mesmerism. James Mowatt, an agnostic up until this time, always included large servings of classical and humanist philosophers in the reading lists he created for her. The enforced exposure to her husband's anti-religious views was intensified when James Mowatt partially lost his vision. Anna Cora would spend hours every day reading his favorite authors aloud to him. Unsurprisingly, Mowatt's "higher self" was quite obsessed with philosophical and religious questions. Unlike her waking personality who did not press her views on anyone, the alternate personality who emerged under hypnosis would confidently argue down all comers. This alternate personality, who called herself the "Gypsy," held views of religion and the afterlife that her auditors found quite similar to those of Emanuel Swedenborg.

Although Mowatt claimed not to have read any of Swedenborg's works prior to her experience with mesmerism, it is not as surprising as it sounds at first that she came up with a parallel vision. Swedenborg was a respected Swedish scientist who late in life began to have visions of the spirit world and write about them. Despite the fact that he died in 1772, he began to have an phenomenal posthumous popularity in the early nineteenth century. His most popular book, *Heaven and Hell*, was available in English in 1772. The Swedish seer's vision of a rational afterlife that was a mirror of bourgeois earthly existence peculiarly fit the intellectual temper of the times. One writer credited the resurgence of popular belief in a spiritual world that is eternal, infinite, primary and the ultimate home of all mortals mainly to Swedenborg.[33] Even disbelieving critics like Ralph Waldo Emerson and Immanuel Kant carried traces of Swedenborg's ideas into their own writings. Writing about Swedenborg's influence, Slater Brown claimed that in the 1830's and 1840's no American author of any account considered himself an informed man of letters unless he could discuss *Heaven and Hell* or other works by Swedenborg with some degree of intelligent understanding.[34] Since James Mowatt saw to it that his wife was very well read, it is not unlikely that while she had not read Swedenborg directly, she had come upon second-hand discussions of his ideas.

There were differences between Mowatt's and Swedenborg's visions as Epes Sargent reports:

> I have spoken, in my account of Mrs. Mowatt of
> her discussions, while somnambulic with Channing,

on the subject of Swedenborg. The great Unitarian divine, while in accord with the Swedish seer on many points, was disposed to question the too human and earth-like character of his descriptions of scenes and occupations in the spirit-world. Mrs. Mowatt defended Swedenborg with discrimination; she admitted that some of his visions were probably subjective and imaginary, but contended that much of his testimony was in accord with the general report which spirits give of the state of things in the next stage of being. She was far from regarding him as infallible. She thought he was in error in describing the Moravians and other Christian dissenters as in a bad state because of their doctrinal tenets. She maintained that the only real heresy was the wrong thinking which led to wrong doing. So long as a man was sincere and pure in heart, his mistakes on doctrinal and historical points could have no serious or permanent effect upon his future happiness.[35]

As it is has been said before, she reflected the views of her mesmerizers who probably led her to some extent with the comments they made and questions they asked. Spiritualists, like Sargent and Channing, had incorporated Swedenborg's outline of a rational spiritual world into their belief system with a few modifications and updates. Like the quibbles Mowatt found with the seer, most spiritualists made changes and exceptions based on humanitarian grounds. Mowatt, however, was not just "preaching to the choir." In her "higher state" she managed to convert one very important doubter in her small audience, James Mowatt. She writes of his change of heart:

Religion was the subject upon which he most frequently dwelt. His mind had naturally a strong skeptical tendency, confirmed by a system of education miscalled philosophical. In what manner his favorite theories were overturned, and his belief in revealed religion established, I do not understand; I only know that there was a downfall of the olden fabric and a foundation laid for the new.[36]

If her experience with mesmerism did nothing else for her, it did help Mowatt find a system of belief upon which both she and her husband could agree. Through the assumed voice of the "Gypsy," Anna Cora also had the opportunity to refute the humanistic views of James Mowatt's that she found most objectionable.

The importance of the mesmeric experiment as an outlet for Mowatt's suppressed voice cannot be understated. She was a brilliant, sensitive and gifted woman in her early twenties at that time, who was treated like a child by the men she respected while in her "normal" state. She reported having the following conversation with Dr. Channing one day:

At last he accosted me with, "Do you understand what you are reading?"

I replied, "I think I do."

"Do you believe it?"

"Yes."

"What makes you believe it?"

"Because I can't help it."

"That's a woman's reason," he answered laughing, "but I believe it is the strongest you could give."[37]

Mowatt reported that on this occasion she was reading Swedenborg's book *Divine Providence*. A passage from that work reads as follows:

> It is known that man has freedom to think and will as he pleases, but not freedom to say whatever he thinks, nor to do whatever he wills. The freedom therefore that is meant is spiritual, and not natural freedom, except when they form one; for to think and will is spiritual, and to speak and act is natural.[38]

This constraint of freedom was true for Mowatt herself. She was free to think as she wished, but was severely restricted by social custom in what she could say or do without incurring censure from her peers. In the alternate state she seemed to have a great deal of hostility towards herself. Sargent wrote:

> Early in my mesmeric experiences with her a puzzle arose which I thus expressed to her while somnambulic: "You always speak of your lower self in the third person, and you never speak of your present self in the first, and you object to being addressed by either your Christian or surname. How shall I call you?" "Call me Gypsy," she replied. "Then I suppose we must give a corresponding name to your waking self. Since she does many things that you disapprove of, suppose we call her simpleton?" So she clapped her hands in glee, and said, "Nothing could be more apt." So the distinctions were adopted, and the two names were ever after seriously used, though not when she was in her normal state.[39]

In her autobiography, Mowatt never referred to these nicknames.

The following formulation of gender-based prejudice from

Swedenborg is typical of this period:

> By some it is also imagined that women are equally capable of elevating the sight of their understanding, into the sphere of light in which men may be, and of viewing things in the same intellectual altitude; an opinion to which they have been led by the writings of certain learned authoresses. But these being examined in their presence in the spiritual world were found to be products not of judgment and wisdom, but of genius and eloquence; and what comes of these two, from elegance and beauty in the style of composition, appears as if it were sublime and erudite,—but only to those who call cleverness wisdom.[40]

This prejudiced view reduces even the most intelligent women to the level of trained animals, deceptively aping the forms used by men to express profound thoughts of which these inferior females were not capable.

Since their culture taught women that they were incapable of profundity, it is not surprising that most women did not try to play demanding intellectual games they could never win. With such a low set of expectations it is no wonder that the men were amazed by the Gypsy's brilliance. They weren't expecting to hear much from a woman. Mowatt herself was not entirely pleased by their preference for this artificial version of herself:

> I was annoyed at being told I had spoken, done, or written things of which I had no recollections. Numerous poems were placed in my hands, which, I was informed, I had improvised as rapidly as they could be taken down, the subject given haphazard by

any person present. It was no particular gratification to be assured that I had never produced anything as good before. Nor was it any consolation to be told than in sleep-walking I was far more sensible, more interesting, and more amiable than in my ordinary state. With womanly perverseness, I preferred my every-day imperfection to this mysteriously and incomprehensibly brought about superiority. For the former I was at least responsible—to the latter I could lay no conscious claim.[41]

As we now suspect, Mowatt could lay a great deal of claim to the things she said or did while under hypnosis. The Gypsy was another manifestation of the imaginative creativity for which she gained fame and fortune. She was simply not getting the proper credit for her work—or for her own natural intelligence.

One thing Mowatt did approve of in her alternate personality was the Gypsy's indomitability:

On one point I felt a degree of satisfaction— though, perhaps it was only proof of my natural obstinacy. They told me that I was what is called an independent somnambulist: and that I could, at any time, defeat the will of the mesmerizer, unless I chose to submit. It was also told me that my reasoning faculties were singularly developed under somnambulism, and I often maintained opinions at variance with those of the mesmerizer or of others with whom I was in communication, especially on religious subjects. These opinions I could not be forced to relinquish by arguments, or even through the exertion of a superior will.[42]

Although the Gypsy was a collaborative creation with men set not only on dominating Mowatt through the exercise of their will, but on subduing the irrational nature of existence into explainable, controllable terms, this alternate personality had a voice of her own. In the social role of the upper-class lady that Mowatt found herself cemented into, she was not free to argue. She could not strike out directly against the narrow-minded friends and family whose disapproval led her to the brink of a nervous breakdown. She could not convince Sargent and Channing to accept her as an intellectual peer. Mowatt could not even get her husband to stop imposing philosophical views on her that she obviously found quite offensive. Mowatt did not have feminism or even an assurance of self-worth independent of her gender to turn to. The only circumstances under which she could freely express herself, defeating the will of those who controlled her, were extraordinary situations where the rules of normal behavior for upper class Victorians were temporarily suspended. Anna Cora Mowatt found covert freedom to speak through the male sanctioned and supervised vehicles of poetry, fiction, theater, and the mesmeric trance.

Mesmerism was a "happy medium" as Mowatt called it. It was a stage where upper class Victorians could ignore temporarily the strict social rules for their social strata and perform experiments testing their social/cultural beliefs. Researchers should not dismiss interest and participation in mesmeric experiments as a mere Victorian oddity, a childish foible of gullible grown-ups. Mesmerism was another form of the private theatrical in which participants dramatically played out suppressed desires and anxieties for their own entertainment and edification. In this and other "strange cases," mesmerism was a performance situation with performance dynamics. Each of the participants played roles and experienced catharsis of some sort. In the case of the mesmerizing of Anna Cora Mowatt, each participant got more from the experiment than he or she might have expected. Epes Sargent found a key to a rational spirit world where science and mysticism were comfortably combined. Dr. Channing obtained convincing proof of his mesmeric powers. James Mowatt discovered a new system of life philosophy. And Anna Cora Mowatt acquired at least temporary relief from a world of frustration and anguish.

CHAPTER 7

**A FAIRY'S DREAM:
SELF-CREATION IN THE POETRY OF
ANNA CORA MOWATT**

Of all things, never may I become that despicable thing, a woman living upon admiration! The village matron, tidying up for her husband and children at evening, is far, far more enviable and respectable.

— Felicia Hemans, poet

In this chapter, I wish to look Anna Cora Mowatt's poems as rhetorical acts of self-fashioning. Mowatt, like almost every other "literary woman" of her era, wrote and published poems. Her works appeared in such popular publications of her day as *The Colombian*, *The Democratic Review*, *The Ladies' Companion*, *Godey's Lady's Book*, and *Graham's Magazine*.[1] For the purposes of this critical view, I am focusing on a single poem with the very autobiographical sounding title, "My Life." Two contemporary anthologists (Griswold and Read) included this poem in collections as one of the best examples of her work.

Despite the fact that she was included in all three of the most prominent collections of works by American women poets of the mid-nineteenth century (Griswold's *Female Poets of America*, Read's *Female Poets of America*, and May's *American Female Poets*), Mowatt did not receive much praise for her poetic works from her critics. Edgar Allan Poe wrote the following summary of her poetic works to date in 1848:

In looking carefully over her poems, I find no one entitled to commendation as a whole; in very few of them do I observe even noticeable passages, and I confess that I am surprised and disappointed at this result of my inquiry; nor can I make up my mind that there is not much latent poetical power in Mrs. Mowatt. From some lines addressed to Isabel M——, I copy the opening stanza as the most favorable specimen which I have seen of her verse:

> *Forever vanished from thy cheek*
> *Is life's unfolding rose;*
> *Forever quenched the flashing smile*
> *That conscious beauty knows!*
> *Thine orbs are lustrous with a light*
> *Which ne'er illumes the eye*
> *Till heaven is bursting on the sight*
> *And earth is fleeting by.*

In this there is much force, and the idea in the concluding quatrain is so well put as to have the air of originality. Indeed, I am not sure that the thought of the last two lines is not original;—at all events it is exceedingly natural and impressive. I say "natural," because, in any imagined ascent from the orb we inhabit, when heaven should "burst on the sight,"—in other words, when the attraction of the planet should be superseded by that of another sphere, then instantly would the "earth" have the appearance of "fleeting by." The versification, also, is much better here than is usual with the poetess. In general she is rough, through excess of harsh consonants. The whole poem is of higher merit than any which I can find with her name attached; but there is little of the spirit of poesy in any thing she writes. She envinces more feeling than ideality.[2]

Poe was not alone in his disappointment. Rufus Griswold, editor of *Female Poets of America*, prefaced the selection of her poems in his collection with the following disparaging comment:

> The poems of Mrs. Mowatt, except *Pelayo* and her dramatic pieces, are brief and fugitive, and generally wanting in that artistic finish of which she has frequently shown herself capable.[3]

Critical reaction to the publication of her long poem *Pelayo*, which Griswold seems to be praising for its length if nothing else, was so adverse that the poetess felt inspired to chide them for their harshness in a rhymed response entitled *Reviewers Reviewed*.

Unlike her novels and plays, there is no evidence that Mowatt's poetry caught the fancy of her reading public, either. Most contemporary and modern biographers omit mention of her poetic works entirely. However, despite this lack of enthusiasm on the part of her public, Mowatt continued to write poetry her entire life. Marius Blesi reports that while she often used pseudonyms in many of her early works, Mowatt habitually published her poems under her own full name.[4] The single important exception to this was the long epic-style romance she titled *Pelayo; or, The Cavern of Covadonga, in Five Cantos*. The poem was her first published work. James Mowatt arranged to have it published in 1836 when Anna Cora was only sixteen.

I believe that Anna Cora Mowatt continued to write and

publish poetry despite the fact that her poetry was not popular because it satisfied various important needs for her. In addition to partially contributing to financial needs, writing poetry helped Mowatt construct a pleasing self for her public and herself. Poetry and the assumed guise of the lady poet aided Mowatt in balancing and justifying her position as being simultaneously a working woman and a woman of sentiment.

In an 1834 editorial for her *American Ladies Magazine*, Sarah Josepha Hale (later to become known for work with *Godey's Lady's Book*) discussed the question of whether or not writing poetry was profitable. The editor was of the opinion that it was not in the monetary sense, but rather in "elevat[ing] our thoughts,... strengthen[ing] our love of the grand, pure and beautiful in art, character and nature," and for "beguiling sorrow, or .. giving pleasure to those we love." This, in Hale's opinion, was poetry's true value and accounted for Hale's extensive use of it in her publications.[5]

Because so many other editors and members of the book buying public shared this valuing of poetry, however, there was a substantial market for poems. Most of the popular magazines of the pre-Civil war era regularly printed poems as fillers between longer fiction and/or non-fictional features. Several of the major newspapers regularly published poems. Not all of these publications paid for such submissions. Most of the more expensive publication did, though. *Graham's Magazine* (for which Edgar Allan Poe served a brief term as literary editor) regularly paid as much as five dollars per poem. William Cullen Bryant and Henry Wadsworth Longfellow, literary "superstars" of the antebellum years, were each offered extravagant fifty dollar per poem contracts to work exclusively for *Graham's*.[6]

From 1817, when *The Literary Gazette* was founded in England, to the outbreak of the Civil War in the United States, publications dedicated to the publication of prose and poetry flourished in both these countries. Angela Leighton, author of

Victorian Women Poets: Writing Against the Heart, attributed the popularity of such publications in England to the fact that they satisfied "the need for a purely literary and popular magazine, free from the political rancors of the main journals, and containing light, readable mixture of poems, stories, letters and fashionable chit chat."[7] I believe the same could be said of a comparable class of American publications which, by and large, vigorously avoided politics. *Godey's Lady's Book*, for example, remained in publication for the entire 1860-1864 period without once mentioning the Civil War. Other than a flourishing of romantic stories and poems about soldiers, the magazine gave no sign the war had occurred.[8]

Poetry, like other forms of literature, served as more than idle entertainment in rapidly growing America, however. Ideals of Jacksonian-style democracy demanded that each citizen be capable of participating fully in government. Proponents of this viewpoint insisted on greater accessibility to education for the general population. Increased public literacy was a goal and subsequently a result of this move. The model citizen/participant in a Jacksonian democracy could not only read well, but should be able to speak well in order to have a voice in government for the people by the people. Educators used poetry, such as Felicia Heman's "Casabianca" (popularly known as "The Boy on the Burning Deck"), to teach students the arts of declamation. Sarah Josepha Hale's familiar "Mary's Lamb" (known now as "Mary Had a Little Lamb") was originally printed in a volume she conceived and designed for younger school children.[9]

As a by-product of increased literacy and aggressive new marketing techniques on the part of American publishers, the so-called "gift book" became popular at this time. These handsomely bound and delicately illustrated volumes were the forerunners of today's coffee table books. Many gift-books were strictly female affairs. In several cases, female editors collected poems by female poets for a readership that they seemed to assume would be predominantly female. *The Ladies' Wreath*, published in Boston by Marsh, Capon and Lyon in 1837 and edited by Sarah Josepha Hale, is somewhat typical of this genre. Hale biographer Isabelle Entrikin described the volume as follows:

> It contained some biographical information ... and some uncritical appreciation of the women included. The work employed the elaborate and artificial device of comparing the poetesses represented to the flowers of a wreath. At the risk of straining the imagination, Joanna Baille was likened to the aloe, Hannah More to the pine, Miss Gould was like the ground laurel, and Mrs. Wells the sweet-briar rose.[10]

As inanely sentimental as the design of the collection might seem, the attitude of the editor was anything but frivolous. Hale wrote a potential publisher that her intentions were to create a work "which will be necessary for every educated lady in our country." She declined to sell the copyright for the volume and demanded a ten per cent premium on the first edition, which she dictated should be a run of not less than two thousand copies.[11]

Although the taste of the times encouraged compositions to be sickly-sweet melodramas of love, the reality of writing for gift-books and the so-called "annuals" was far from romantic. Often it required hard-headed composition to meet strict deadlines. In *Victorian Women Poets*, Angela Leighton related the story of a certain Miss Mitford, editor of an English publication called *Finden's Tableaux*, who once wrote Elizabeth Barrett Browning to request a poem illustrating "a very charming group of Hindoo girls floating their lamps upon the Ganges." It was a common practice for annuals to first obtain illustrations and then commission poems to go along with them. This particular poem, Miss Mitford went further to specify, should be written in stanzas and long enough for two large pages. She requested the poem be completed within two to three weeks. In just two weeks, Leighton reports, Barrett Browning produced the twenty-three stanzas of "A Romance of the Ganges."[12]

Although women in preceding centuries had written poems and some had even written for financial reward, the woman poet as a self-professed and self-supporting writer appears, almost for the first time in history, in the post-Romantic decades of the 1820s and 30s.[13]   Caroline May prefaces her 1848 collection of poems by American women by saying:

> One of the most striking characteristics of the present age is the number of female writers, especially in the department of *belles-lettres*. This is even more true of the United States, than of the old world; and poetry, which is the language of affections, has been freely employed among us to express the emotions of a woman's heart.
>
> Few American women, besides the author of *Zophiel*, have written poems of any considerable length, but many have published volumes of poetry, and fugitive pieces of various merit have been poured forth through our newspapers and other periodicals, with the utmost profusion.[14]

Unlike other literary fields, women like Anna Cora Mowatt who were protective of their social status comfortably affixed their full legal names to their poetic work. Lady's magazines, gift books and annuals offered a context for publication which, being largely female, presupposed a kind of literary modesty while at the same time offered a discreetly lucrative living.

A cultural mystique grew around the figure of the woman

poet at this time, offering, as Leighton points out, subsequent generations of women "both an enthusiastic incentive to write and a subtly determining myth of what being a woman poet means."[15] An important part of this myth was that women's poetry was primarily an effusion, a spontaneous flow of feeling onto the page. This idea was an extension of the picture of the ideal woman of sensibility, a creature of pure, true, but largely unreflective and uncritical emotion.

A critic responding to a volume of Felicia Heman's work in 1847 wrote approvingly:

> Mrs. Heman's poems are strictly effusions. And not a little of their charm springs from their unstudied and extempore character. This, too, is in fine keeping with the sex of the writer. You are saved the ludicrous image of a double dyed Blue, in papers and morning wrapper, sweating at some stupendous treatise or tragedy from morn to noon, and from noon to dew—you see a graceful and gifted woman, passing from the cares of her family, and the enjoyments of society, to inscribe on her tablets some fine thought or feeling, which had throughout the day existed as a still sunshine upon her countenance, or perhaps as a quiet unshed tear in her eye. In this case, the transition is so natural and graceful, from the duties or delights of the day to the employments of the desk, that there is as little pedantry in writing a poem as in writing a letter...[16]

The seeming ease with which the critic imagined the poem was composed was at least as important as the content. As you may remember, Anna Cora Mowatt's friends thought the poetry that Mowatt's mesmeric alter ego, "the Gypsy," extemporized on their command better than anything she had ever written in her waking state.[17] This preference, which Mowatt seemed to find puzzling and a little offensive, could also have sprung from similar valuing of spontaneous ease of composition over actual content.

The praise one finds by critics and auditors lauding the qualities that contribute to what Heman's critic called the "unstudied and extempore character" of women's poetry, clearly shows a favoring of work that gives the appearance of having been written with no intellectual effort. As Leighton pointed out, this imagined "extempore mode" supports the ideal of a woman as "unselfish, unthinking and sexually appealing, and thus, in spite of all that housework, aristocratically redundant in relation to the intellectual work force." The verse of this culturally created vision of the ideal poetess is, Leighton continued, "like a smile on her face or a tear in her eye, unconsciously and spontaneously physiological, but neither sweaty or ungraceful."[18] The woman poet, therefore, despite the hard-nosed realities of her craft, became in the popular imagination not a new class of working woman but rather an object of conspicuous sentimentality; usually, as Leighton put it, "tearful herself and provoking tears in her reader."[19]

This close correspondence between the ideal nature of the sentimental woman and the effusiveness of women's poetry made such poetry and poets artistically suspect, however. Compiler Rufus Griswold skeptically prefaced his *Female Poets of America*, with the following:

> It is less easy to be assured of the genuineness of literary ability in women than in men. The moral nature of women, in its finest and richest development, partakes some of the qualities of genius; it assumes, at least, the similitude of that which in men is the characteristic accompaniment of the highest grade of mental inspiration. We are in danger, therefore, of mistaking for the efflorescent energy of

creative intelligence, that which is only the exuberance of personal "feelings unemployed." We may confound the vivid dreaming of an unsatisfied heart with the aspirations of a mind impatient of the fetters of time, matter, and mortality. That may seem to us the abstract imagining of a soul rapt into sympathy with a purer beauty and a higher truth than earth and space exhibit, which in fact shall be only the natural craving of affections, undefined and wandering. The most exquisite susceptibility of the spirit, and the capacity to mirror in dazzling variety the effects which circumstances or surrounding minds work upon it, may be accompanied by no greater power to originate, nor even, in any proper sense, to reproduce. It does not follow, because the most essential genius in men is marked by qualities which we may call feminine, that such qualities when found in female writers have any certain or just relation to mental superiority.[20]

Griswold's preface encapsulates the separate set of assumptions a sentimentalist carried into reading women's poetry. Unfair as it might have been, this double standard opened the door for women's poetry to exist. Because effusive poetry was considered by the sentimentalist as a natural outpouring of the ideal woman of sentiment, poetesses were not considered unnatural. Because their poetry was considered effortless sentiment rather than intellectual labor, women artists were also taken safely out of competition with men.

Anna Cora Mowatt made almost no mention of her mature poetry or her image of herself as an adult poet in her autobiography. She did, however, relate the following story about her first encounter with poetry and experimentations with being a poet. Several references embedded in this narrative conform to the effusive ideal for women poets:

Of poetry I never tired, and at ten years old I had read the whole of Shakespeare's plays many times over. My reading was not guided—I was allowed to take any book that I chose, French or English from my father's library. When I look back upon some of the works which I perused with avidity at that early age, I can hardly believe it possible that a child could have waded through them, or culled out meaning enough to render the subjects interesting. I amused myself by writing also, and fancied that I wrote poetry, because I made the ends of lines rhyme. Every marriage, or birth, or death, or exciting circumstance that occurred in the family invariably furnished me with a subject. All my deeper feelings spontaneously expressed themselves in verse. I used to sit for hours stringing doggerel together, and longing to show it to somebody who would be sure to say that the verses were very beautiful. I seldom had courage to exhibit these infantile productions, but laid little plots to secure their being seen. Sometimes I would leave a copy of verses on the floor in some of my brothers' rooms, or on the nursery mantelpiece, or write them on the walls in the garden, which at one period were covered over with rhymes. I seldom got praised for any of these effusions, and I doubt whether they deserved any praise; though I, at the time, imagined them very fine. One day I let fall a little "poem"—as I designated it— in the room of one of my brothers, and soon after perceived him coming out of his apartment with the paper in his hand. He went downstairs, and, unperceived, I stole softly after him. When he entered the drawing room, where my father was sitting, I dropped down on the last step with my heart beating so painfully that I could scarcely breathe. I could hear him say, "Just read this, papa; it is some of Anna's nonsense."

I sat still, too much agitated to move, but not able to overhear what passed, until the words came to me in my father's voice, "I wish you would call her."

I sprang up to betake myself to flight; but my brother had opened the door before I could disappear. I was summoned. I entered the room like a culprit who had been guilty of some heavier crime than that of murdering English and perpetrating bad poetry.

"Did you write these lines yourself?" inquired my father, in his usual kind tone.

"Yes," I answered.

"Are you sure nobody helped you? Are you sure that you did not get them out of some book?"

I replied, indignantly, that they were my own. I was beginning to be elated by the idea that probably I had produced something wonderful, after all.

"They are not very good grammar," said my father; "but they are quite pretty, for all that. Who knows what my little chicken may turn out one of these days?" he added, caressing me.

These were the first words of praise that had ever been bestowed upon what I wrote. I felt inclined to cry for joy; but my brother took the lines, and began pointing out the flagrant mistakes in metre, in grammar, in sense; and I snatched the paper out of his hand and ran away. My childish heart was full of conflicting emotions—delight at my father's approval—vexation with my brother—shame at my own ignorance in writing so incorrectly. For a long period after that I kept everything I wrote carefully locked up, and made a bonfire when my store accumulated beyond bounds.[21]

Mowatt's picture of herself as child poet and lover of poetry is consistent with the popular image of the ideal poetess.

Biographers record similar poetic prodigy in the lives of more famous contemporary female poets such as Felicia Hemans, Letitia Elizabeth Landon, and Elizabeth Barrett Browning. Coming at such an early age, the inclination to poetry is spontaneous and unprompted. Their precocious urge to write is natural and irrepressible. The emphasis by biographers and autobiographers on youthful forays into poetry locate the wellsprings of such women's poetic ability at the site of childish emotionalism rather than mature reflection.

The poetess as imagined by her culture also had her dark side. Madame de Stael's popular novel *Corinne: or Italy* told the story of a poetess who gains worldly fame but ends up dying from grief when she loses her lover to a more domesticated woman. The Corinne story reverberates endlessly through the lives and works of nineteenth century poetesses. The image of Corinne haunts the life stories of women poets as well as popping up periodically in their poetry. Poetesses, as they were portrayed by their contemporary biographers, either lived their lives in stern denial of their worldly success or seemed to fall inexorably into Corinne's tragic pattern of decay and death. Lady poets of the first half of the nineteenth century also enthusiastically embraced the myth of a heterosexualized Sappho, who at the height of her creative powers committed suicide because of her unrequited love for the boatman Phaon. In either of these tales the cautionary message is clear: a woman's creative success leads to moral and domestic disaster.

Although it was culturally acceptable for ladies to write poetry, this dark side of the mystique of the poetess implicitly indicates such a career was not an entirely safe venture. In both their poetry and the public personas they created, poetesses struggled to maintain strong ties to home, hearth and other conventional symbols of femininity. In *American Female Poets*, editor Caroline May offers a conventional contemporary explanation of the prevalence of domestic themes in women's poetry:

> It must be borne in mind that not many ladies in this country are permitted sufficient leisure from the cares and duties of home to devote themselves, either from choice, or as a means of living, to literary pursuits. Hence, the themes which have suggested the greater part of the poems have been derived from the incidents and associations of every-day life. And home, with its quiet joys, its deep pure sympathies, and its secret sorrows, with which a stranger must not intermeddle, is a sphere by no means limited for a woman, whose inspiration lies more in her heart than her head.[22]

I argue that since May was speaking about the few American ladies that *did* have enough time to devote themselves to writing poetry as an avocation or a profession, the picture she painted of the lady poetess tending her household while she composes is a misleading one. In many cases, the homey flavor of women's poetry reflected the experiences and expectations poetesses imagined of their audiences far more than such domesticity reflected the day-to-day life of the poetess.

Despite the way the fiction of the "effusive mode" of women's poetry kept poetesses in line with conventional expectations of womanly sensibility, women poets were still women of middle or upper class backgrounds independently earning a living outside their homes. Their occupation put them outside previously defined boundaries of what it meant to be proper middle or upper class ladies. If a poetess failed to maintain the charade of conventionality, she ran the danger of becoming an outcast, a fate as ultimately tragic as that of Corinne, Sappho, the lady of Shallot, and Mariana combined.

It is possible to interpret Mowatt's poem, "My Life," in such a way that the tensions inherent in the life of a woman of sensibility living in the public sphere runs through the text as an undercurrent.   The text appears as follows in both Griswold's and Read's collections:

My Life.

My life is a fairy's gay dream,
And thou art the genii, whose wand
Tints all things around with the beam,
The bloom of Titania's bright land.
A wish to my lips never sprung,
A hope in mine eyes never shone,
But, ere it was breathed by my tongue,
To grant it thy footsteps have flown.
Thy joys, they have ever been mine,
Thy sorrows, too often thine own;
The sun that on me still would shine,
O'er thee threw its shadows alone.
Life's garland then let us divide,
Its roses I'd fain see thee wear,
For one—but I know thou wilt chide —
Ah! leave me its thorns, love, to bear![23]

The words alone of this poem by no means mandate an autobiographical interpretation.   The non-gendered speaker merely proclaims his or her gratitude to an auditor for the generous contributions he or she has made or is making to the speaker's life, hinting that the listener has shielded the speaker from unspecified pain.   The speaker offers to atone by accepting the listener's share of suffering as well as his or her own. The modern reader is left free to impose any combination of genders on the poem's characters. The text could as easily be a male addressing a female or another male as it could be a female addressing a male or another female. A reader could imagine a child speaking the words of the poem to an adult as easily as an adult speaking them to a child.

However in the nineteenth century, long before Barthes proclaimed the death of the author as an entity for critical consideration, readers assumed the speaker of a poem to be the poet unless the poem was clearly in the dramatic mode (such as Robert Browning's "My Last Duchess"). Since Mowatt gives us no overt indications that she means the poem to be taken otherwise, let us take the title's implied invitation and impose an autobiographical frame on the poem. If the speaker is Mowatt herself and the listener is either of the two publicly acknowledged most important men in her life, her father or her husband, the poem turns into a successful woman apologizing to a man for her success. The speaker of the poem attributes her prosperity not to her own efforts but to the magnanimity of the listener. The speaker describes her life as a "fairy's gay dream." Fairies, in folklore as well as in Shakespeare's "Midsummer Night's Dream," referred to in line four, are known to play tricks on human beings. Saying, "My life is a fairy's gay dream" could be interpreted to mean "My life is beautiful and fantastic" or "My life is like the sort of a prank a fairy might conceive to play on my vanity." In either case, the speaker's life is characterized as something beautiful, but unreal and unnatural.

If one accepts my autobiographical interpretation, the poem tends to indicate that Mowatt felt guilt and regret over outshining her mentor. The fact that the person she addresses has not been at least equally successful spoils her enjoyment of her fame. This guilt prevents her from standing boldly on the steps of the capitol like de Stael's Corinne and accepting the laurels of her own artistic triumph. Her ties to her mentor, who represents her home, keep her humble, but also keep her safe from the sort of death and despair that are the traditional fate of the outcast woman artist.

As I said before, nothing in the words of the poem itself demands such an interpretation from the reader. For a piece entitled "My Life," the poem is surprisingly impersonal. There were advantages to this sort of textual ambiguity for a sentimental lady poet. To begin with, critics seemed to admire and encourage a strict adherence to established poetic forms from poetesses. Rufus Griswold, in his preface to *Female Poets*, indicated his preference for disciplined creativity in women:

> Among men, we recognize his nature as the most thoroughly artist-like, whose most abstract thoughts still retain a sensuous cast, whose mind is the most completely transfused and incorporated into his feelings. Perhaps the reverse should be considered the test of a true art in a woman, and we should deem her the truest poet, whose emotions are the most refined by reason, whose force of passion is most expanded and controlled into lofty and impersonal forms of imagination.[24]

Mowatt, in a manner that must have pleased Griswold, employed a number of conventional Victorian poetic devices that distance "My Life" from reality. The poem's strict *abab* rhyme scheme gives it a predictable, almost sing-song quality that holds the reader at arm's length. Although male poets experimented with other rhythmic patterns at this time, Mowatt, like most poetesses, still used rigid traditional rhyme schemes. As Leighton put it, "moral as well as metrical regularity was preferred in women."[25]

Archaic language such as the persistent use of "thee" and "thy" displaces the poem from a Victorian timeframe. In addition, calling the characters fairies or genii keeps their identity neutral and nongender specific as well as located in a misty mythic past. Such intertextual references pull the reader away from a strictly specific and personal interpretation by placing the poem in a larger literary context. In the following poem, which also appears in Griswold's collection, Mowatt used archaic language and literary references to an even greater extent:

Love

Thou conqueror's conqueror, mighty Love! to thee
Their crowns, their laurels, kins and heroes yield;
Lo! at thy shrine great Antony bows the knee,
Disdains his victor's wreath, and flies the field!
From woman's lips Alcides lists thy tone,
And grasps the inglorious distaff for his sword.
An eastern sceptre at thy feet is thrown,
A nation's worshipped idol owns thy lord;
And well fair Noorjehan his throne became,
When erst she ruled his empire in thy name.

The sorcerer Jarchas could to age restore
Youth's faded bloom or childhood's vanished glee;
Magician Love! canst thou not yet do more?
Is not the faithful heart kept young by thee?
But ne'er that traitor-bosom formed to stray,
Those perjured lips which twice thy vows have breathed,
Can know the raptures of thy magic sway,
Or find the balsam in thy garland wreathed;
Fancy or Folly may his breast have moved,
But he who wanders never truly loved.[26]

More so than in "My Life," Mowatt ventriloquized Shakespere in "Love" to the point that the poem becomes completely detached from Mowatt's own lifetime.

As I mentioned before, Mowatt gave no identification of either the speaker or the person being addressed. The speaker addresses the listener as "love" at one point, but other than that, the speaker discusses their relationship in a series of metaphors.

Mowatt substitutes sentimental shorthand such as "life's garland" and "hope in my eyes" for references to real events.

Cliches also fill "On a Lock of My Mother's Hair," a poem that Mowatt wrote shortly after her mother's death.

On a Lock of My Mother's Hair

Whose the eyes thou erst didst shade,
Down what bosom hast thou rolled,
O'er what cheek unchidden played,
Tress of mingled brown and gold!
Round what brow, say, didst thou twine?

Angel-mother, it was thine!
Cold the brow that wore this braid,
Pale the cheek this bright lock pressed,
Dim the eyes it loved to shade,
Still the ever-gentle breast —
All that bosom's struggles past,
When it held this ringlet last.

In that happy home above,
Where all perfect joy hath birth,
Thou dispensest good and love,
Mother, as thou didst on earth.
And though distant seems that sphere,
Still I feel thee ever near.

Though my longing eye now views
Thy angelic mien no more,
Still thy spirit can infuse
Good in mine, unknown before.
Still the voice, from childhood dear,
Steals upon my raptured ear —
Chiding every wayward deed,

> Fondly praising every just,
> Whispering soft, when strength I need,
> "Loved one! place in God thy trust!"
> Oh, 'tis more than joy to feel
> Thou art watching o'er my weal![27]

Despite the emotional subject of "On a Lock of My Mother's Hair," the proliferation of sentimental metaphors that were well-worn even a century and a half ago gives the poem a flat, lifeless quality. As Edgar Allan Poe pointed out in his critique of her poetry, Mowatt seemed more adept at stringing popular sentimental images together than at creating original ones. The use of metaphor keeps the emotional message of "On a Lock of My Mother's Hair" and "My Life" nonspecific and impersonal despite their autobiographical content.

Ambiguity, in addition to keeping the poem from a "womanly" nonuniversality her critics might find distasteful, preserves Mowatt's privacy. Although she titled the poem "My Life," any correspondence to her own life readers may read into it is conjecture. Even if we are bold enough to assume that Mowatt is the speaker, she does not embarrass the less successful listener addressed in the poem by giving away any clues to his/her identity. Under the guise of poetic ambiguity, Mowatt may, or may not, be discussing in this poem the emotional trauma of a situation both novel and unacceptable to many of her contemporaries—a middle to upper class working wife supporting her less capable husband.

Although Anna Cora Mowatt was not thought of by anyone, perhaps not even herself, as a particularly gifted poet, I believe she continued to write poetry because it was an inviting medium for a number of reasons. Poetry brought in cash. Critics might not have thought much of her verses, but editors published them. The financial compensation might not have been impressive, but every little bit helped the often financially-strapped Mowatts.

Most importantly, the lady poet, unlike lady novelist or lady playwright, was a culturally accepted role for a woman of sentiment. Mowatt made more money from her novels and plays, but always seemed uneasy and apologetic about her lucrative trespasses into these traditionally masculine literary territories. The excerpt from her autobiography testifies that Mowatt's father encouraged her to experiment with poetry. Her father's approval was extremely important and empowering to Mowatt. She put more weight on the judgment of her personal patriarch than she did on the opinions of her patriarchal culture as a whole. Finally, the impersonal, ambiguous style favored by critics for women poets of the first few decades of the nineteenth century allowed Mowatt to pour out what she called her "deeper feelings" without threatening her privacy or the privacy of those she cared for.

In short, poetry was power—the power to earn money, the power to speak, and the power to conceal. Mowatt did not write poetry that was great in any of the ways people usually judge greatness in poems. Her poems did not transcend her own time. She did not use language in a unique or innovative way. She did not poignantly address what others define as the great social issues of her time. Mowatt did, however, write poems that were acceptable—to her culture, her critics, and herself.

CHAPTER 8

"AND EARTH IS FLEETING BY:" REFLECTIONS ON THE LEGACY OF ANNA CORA MOWATT

In a time when society strictly limited the range of roles a woman was free to play without losing her status as a lady, Anna Cora Mowatt was an author, public reader, playwright, actress, poet and novelist. She was a well-known and respected figure among her contemporaries in American literary and dramatic circles. Critics and historians have identified her as a significant and influential figure.

Arthur Hobson Quinn, when summarizing her achievements, enthusiastically stated:

> Real as her contribution to our drama was, her influence upon our theater was probably even greater. Coming into a life which, notwithstanding the many sterling men and women who pursued it, still suffered from the traditions of loose standards and the disapproval of the Puritan element in our society, she proved triumphantly that an American gentlewoman could succeed in it without the alteration of her own standard of life. She took into the profession her high heart, her utter refinement, her keen sense of social values, and her infinite capacity for effort, and her effect was a real and great one. She met the half-concealed jealousy of the British companies with

which she acted with that disarming courtesy which the highbred of her nation have perhaps known best how to employ, and her career as retold in the steady spark of her *Autobiography* makes any compatriot who reads it thankful that she has lived.[1]

Quinn felt that as a respectable woman in a career that was considered dubious by many, Mowatt helped turn the tide of feeling against theater in mid-century America.

Less enthusiastically, theater historian Laurence Hutton, writing in 1891, blamed Mowatt's example for the large influx of society ladies with no background in theater who entered the acting profession during his day:

> There have been debutantes enough in New York since the debut of Mrs. Mowatt to fill to overflowing the auditorium of any single city theater, could they be gathered under one roof to witness the first effort of the next aspirant, whoever she may be. During the season of 1876-77 alone, not less than seven ladies— Mrs. Louise M. Pomeroy, Miss Bessie Darling, Miss Anna Dickinson, Mrs. J.H. Hackett, Miss Minnie Cummings, Miss Marie Wainwright, and Miss Adelaide Lennox—in leading parts made their first bows to metropolitan audiences, without training or experience; and the season was not considered a particularly strong one in debutantes at that. For much of this Mrs. Mowatt, unconsciously and unwittingly was responsible. Her sudden success turned many heads, while the equally sudden failures, not recorded, but very many in number, have been quite forgotten, and will be still ignored as long as there are new Camilles and new Juliets to achieve greatness at one fell swoop, and as long as there are

unwise friends and speculative managers to encourage them.[2]

It was his opinion that the seeming effortlessness of Mowatt's success as an actress encouraged other amateurs from her class to try a stage career. Unstated but implicit in his evaluation is an echoing of Quinn's assumption that Mowatt's example made the career of actress a viable option for a woman of her class.

Mowatt herself reported that her one season of public readings in 1841-42 immediately inspired many imitators:

> My success gave rise to a host of lady imitators, one of whom announced "Readings and Recitations in the Style of Mrs. Mowatt." I was rather curious to get an idea of my own style, and, had my health permitted, would have gone some distance to have seen it illustrated. At one time there were no less than six advertisements in the papers, of ladies giving readings in different parts of the Union.[3]

Although it is nearly impossible to determine to what extent any or all of the above writers were guilty of engaging in *post hoc ergo propter hoc* reasoning, the weight of opinion suggests that Mowatt was a potent role model.[4]

Mowatt was a significant figure not only for the uniqueness of her contribution to any one creative field, but rather for the variety of her achievements. Female contemporaries may have gained more fame and recognition as actresses, novelists, or poets, but no other woman of America's mid-nineteenth century could boast of comparable success in a similarly wide range of fields. Anna Cora Mowatt took advantage of and achieved a measure of success in a variety of creative media open to her.

Mowatt's works—non-fiction, prose fiction, plays, performance, and poetry—are significant not only because of their variety but also because of their cumulative creation of a consistent and viable public voice. Mowatt created and defended her discursive authority in various and sophisticated manners.

Anna Cora Mowatt's tightrope walk between pleasing herself and pleasing society is a story that resonates with the concerns of women today. Her struggle for credibility reflected the questions of her times about the respectability of creative women and the ability of any individual to lead an honest and respectable life in a public realm where deceit is necessary for survival. Her success mirrored the success that her contemporaries wished to have in striking the right balance between being sincere and being "savvy."

In her introduction to *Fictions of Authority*, Susan Lanser states that before anyone can speak with true authority about woman writers and the strategies they employ to establish an authoritative voice, many more studies of women's texts from many different cultures and from many different vantage points must be done.[5] This book is one of what I hope will be many answers to Lanser's call. Although Lanser was speaking only of how women created authority for themselves in writing fiction, Mowatt's life and various works established discursive authority in many creative forms. When considered as one meta-text, Mowatt's various works function together to work towards the goal of creating discursive authority without sacrificing her position as a lady.

In order to succeed in her quest for discursive authority without sacrificing her status as a lady, Mowatt had to engage in a constant process of negotiation, sometimes even involving the simultaneous playing of conflicting roles. Because "ladies" were not supposed even to desire to be active in the public realm, appearing on the stage involved the breaking of stronger social taboos than such a career choice signaled for men of that time. Therefore a woman's involvement in theater required greater justification and explanation. Such a choice put a woman like Anna Cora Mowatt into an uncertain and precarious social position. For actresses, this division between public and private selves was especially troublesome because of their high visibility.

Regardless of how widely her contemporaries shared this constricting view of actresses in society, it is clear that Mowatt perceived that going on stage was a dangerous choice. Her fears are clear in the following scene she presented in her autobiography:

It was the most trying duty to make my intended debut known to my family. My sister May was, of course, the first in whom I confided. She was of a gentle and timid nature, and shrank in alarm from the proposed public step. She could not discuss it without tears and violent emotion.

"You cannot go through with it—I am sure you cannot!" were her weeping exclamations.

"We none know what we can do until we are tried," was the truism with which I answered her objection.

"What will our friends say of you if you make a public appearance?" she urged.

"What will our friends do for us in case I do not? Will they preserve to us this sweet home? Will they support us? Will they even sympathize with our adversity?"

"But you will lose your position in society."

"If I fail, probably I shall; but I do not intend to fail. And what is that position in society worth when we are no longer able to feast and entertain? How many of those whom we feasted and entertained at our last ball will seek us out when we live in poverty and obscurity?"

"If you would only look at all the obstacles!"

"No, I am looking above and beyond them, and I see only duty in their place."[6]

This emotional scene between the two sisters demonstrates Mowatt's perception of the danger she risked to her reputation by assuming the role of actress. She decided to go on with her plans despite these dangers—not because they were not real to her.

Mowatt was forced, therefore, in her autobiography and other works to negotiate her relationship with the theater in order to be accepted simultaneously as an actress, playwright and a lady. She was careful about the way she presented herself as well as her desires and motivations. She stressed her aversion to acting so much that Mildred Butler was moved to call her Mowatt biography *An Actress in Spite of Herself.* Despite these protestations, Mowatt herself reports that she exhibited a passion for theatrical entertainments when she was little more than an infant. She wrote plays before she had seen the inside of a theater. She acted in amateur productions from the time she was able to speak.

Mowatt was a person who had exhibited a strong affinity for the theatrical from an early age. In reporting such childish tendencies, however, Mowatt tended to use them as idyllic examples of family togetherness rather than as pre-professional training. What is not stressed in such accounts was how elaborate and well-attended these "childish" pastimes were. She won her first writing job from a periodical editor who attended one such event. Mowatt dismissed these family performances as the foibles of youth. She made her decision to go into the theater in the small, semi-respectable channel of public reading, she insisted, not because of her great interest in theater, but to help her poor husband.

When recounting her decision to go on the stage, Mowatt emphasized her good qualities of wifely duty and suffering and downplayed any unacceptable exhibitionist desires she may have felt herself. When she recorded herself as exclaiming (in a nobly melodramatic fashion that would also have fallen well from the lips of *Fashion*'s Adam Trueman or Gertrude), she painted the onset of her stage career not as the satisfaction of base desires for fame and recognition, but as a noble quest:

> If I fail, probably I shall; but I do not intend to fail! And what is that position in society worth when we are no longer able to feast and entertain? How many of those whom we feasted and entertained at our last ball will seek us out when we live in poverty and obscurity?[7]

She portrayed herself as a "lady" who must defy prudishness and suffer the condemnation of her peers in order to save her home.

Mowatt carefully let her audiences know that she did not go on the stage to make herself happy, but instead risked her reputation and good health for the institutions of home and husband so dear to the heart of any true woman of sentiment. Mowatt thus negotiated her role as a successful moneymaker in a masculine world with her acceptance of patriarchal conventions. She carefully recorded herself playing the parts of dutiful wife and daughter in her writing. Because of her compliance to conventional expectations in these and other symbolic traditional relationships to men, she was able to exploit her submissiveness and use the authority of her husband, her father and other approving male figures to authorize her unlady-like roles.

In her autobiography, Mowatt acknowledged the possible

negative interpretations of her actions. She included a report that many of her critics and her friends went so far as to question whether or not her husband had actually lost any money. The majority of critics, however, were either convinced of her honesty or charmed enough by her persona to let her claims go unquestioned. Mowatt created a narrative voice that readers could feel comfortable indulging with their attention and crafted a narrative framework for her life story that was familiar to her auditors. In the absence of an appropriate pattern for women's life stories, Mowatt borrowed from popular fiction and skillfully employed narrative devices that enhanced her credibility as a speaker by underplaying the aggressive unconventionality of her life story. In this non-fictive work, Mowatt wooed her suspicious public by fashioning a self that was not proud, self-aggrandizing, or threateningly unfeminine.

In *Mimic Life*, she continued her fight against what she considered the ignorant and unreflective anti-theatrical bias in her society. However, under the authorial mask, she was a step further removed from her imagined audience in this fictive work. In her *Autobiography*, she had to negotiate the responsibilities of both the role of creator and subject. In *Mimic Life*, she was playing only the role of creator. This narrowing of her role and the fictive format left Mowatt free to vilify the anti-theatrical prejudice. For example, in her *Autobiography*, Mowatt was constrained as to how disrespectful she could be in her description of Rev. Eastburn or how immodest she could be in portraying herself. However, because the characters in *Mimic Life* were fictions rather than real people, Mowatt was free to make protagonist Tina Trueheart as angelic and her nemesis Miss Haughtonville as obnoxious as she wished without risking her discursive authority.

Mowatt's hit comedy *Fashion* was itself a negotiation of her relationship to theater and to society. Although much of the public disdained theater itself, theatricality and guise were paradoxically becoming a less feared aspect of private life. Sentimentality, though it celebrated the natural and the pure, engendered great theatricality. Affecting the idealized reactions privileged by the sentimentalists required great skill. The unexpected success of Mowatt's *Fashion* was a testament to the growing awareness of and tolerance for theatricality as it was manifest in social life. Much of the comedy of the play depends on an ability to identify inappropriate tactics of self-promotion. Rather than condemning such deceptive behavior entirely, in the way a work from an earlier period of American history might have done, the play encourages audience members to look at such behavior in a milder and less judgmental light. The play's Tiffany family are not dangerous confidence men to be feared and shunned because of their desire to deceive, but are presented as comically inept bunglers in the gentle art of creating the illusion of being persons of high society.

Mowatt's attack on social theatricality was itself presented within a theatrical performance. The tensions and contradictions of attempting to act out the role of the honest and sincere citizen that the sentimentalists idolized without resorting to pretense had loosened enough by this time to enable audiences to laugh at the attempts of fictional others to establish and maintain a desirable social persona.

The theater, while still held in contempt as a profession by many people, slowly gained recognition as a workable metaphor for social behavior. Thus to an anxious American public learning the game of impression management, Anna Cora Mowatt had the potential to be a role model instead of a "fallen woman." Mowatt's created public persona was that of a person of gentle sentiment who was worthy of trust and respect. The careful manner in which she exhibited appropriate behavior and explained in acceptable ways her deviant behavior prevented her from being cast out and condemned as a painted hussy showing herself for money, but rather caused her to be admired as a successful mistress of the genteel art of self-presentation. Through this skillful manipulation of her public's expectations and assumptions, Mowatt was able to maintain the approval of her peers despite her unconventionality. Unlike other actresses who were admired but not respected, Mowatt was able to work just far enough within the framework of her society's expectations to be considered a lady while doing exactly what she wanted.

Mowatt's experience with mesmerism is an example of the sort of private theatricals in which she and contemporaries engaged—even though mesmerism was not overtly acknowledged as performance. Her private performances under hypnosis were part of Mowatt's negotiations with repressive conventional notions of correct behavior for upper-class American women of the early nineteenth century. While in the character of the "Gypsy," Mowatt could ignore temporarily the strict social rules of her social strata and perform experiments testing her social/cultural limits. The unreal Gypsy was free within the experimental context of mesmeric sessions to give vent to the full range of Mowatt's intelligence, aggression, and rebellion. Mowatt was, under this guise, able to persuade her husband to abandon his anti-religious beliefs and to impress Epes Sargent, Dr. Channing and unnamed others with the full, unfettered creative and intellectual power of her mind. None of these displays of unfeminine forcefulness threatened her role as lady because mesmerism was not seen as real life. Although the arguments she made as "the Gypsy" had persuasive impact on her auditors that changed their relationship with Anna Cora, because such things were said within a performance setting, Mowatt was not obliged to take any responsibility for them.

Mowatt's poems were also part of her negotiations with her culture. The lady poet, unlike lady novelist or lady playwright, was a culturally accepted role for a woman of sentiment. Mowatt made more money from her novels and plays, but always seemed uneasy and apologetic about her lucrative trespasses into these traditionally masculine literary territories. The lady poet unlike the lady playwright or lady novelist did not violate the boundaries of what was culturally considered male literary territory. As Mowatt vigorously attempted to do in her forays into other fields of artistic endeavor, the poetess could express herself publicly without automatically sacrificing her position as a lady. The metaphor-laden, ambiguous language common in women's poetry of this Post-Romantic age allowed the poetess to express deep feelings without necessarily making her social criticisms sharp or revealing many hard facts about herself. Mowatt's most subtle and elusive creations of self are in her poetry.

Mowatt was successful in her quest to create through rhetorical/textual strategies an authoritative voice in her varied works. Moreover she was successful in her efforts to establish such a voice for herself without disqualifying herself to be considered a lady. To accomplish this feat, Mowatt had to fashion a public voice for herself without appearing to her auditors to be in any way immoral or a cunning, manipulative, usurper of masculine power.

The first category of evidence that I offer as proof of her success seems like a rather weak one on the surface. I argue that Anna Cora Mowatt was successful in establishing and maintaining her position as a lady because there are no statements to the contrary from her contemporaries. Given the vagaries and conventions of history writing, this absence hardly seems conclusive. However, one must bear in mind that in claiming to be a *lady* rather than simply a woman of good character, Mowatt was making an assertion that invited dispute.

The following excerpt from Marion Harland's autobiography clearly alludes to the sort of rigorous criterion to which such a claim was subject:

[William Foushee Ritchie] brought [Anna Cora] to quiet Richmond, and installed her in a modest cottage on our side of the town, but three blocks from my father's house. The Ritchies were one of the best of our oldest families; Mrs. Mowatt belonged to one as excellent; her character was irreproachable. I recollect Doctor Haxall insisting upon this when a very conservative Mrs. Grundy "wondered if we ought to visit her."

"You will see, madam, that she will speedily be as popular here as she has been elsewhere. She is a lovely woman, and as to reputation—hers is irreproachable—absolutely! No tongue has ever wagged against her."

I listened with curiosity that had not a tinge of personal concern in it. It went without saying that an ex-actress was out of my sphere. The church that condemned dancing was yet more severe upon the theater. True, Mrs. Ritchie had left the stage, and, it was soon bruited abroad, never recited except in her own home and in the fine old colonial homestead of Brandon, where lived Mr. Ritchie's sister, Mrs. George Harrison. But she had trodden the boards for eight or nine years, and that stamped her as a personage quite unlike the rest of "us."[8]

To be a lady, from Harland's account, one had to be of an "excellent" family and of "irreproachable" character. No scandal could be attached to a lady's name. Mowatt's conservative Richmond neighbors seemed from Harland's account to be actively searching for evidence of inappropriate behavior from Anna Cora. That Mowatt was within the next two years not only to overcome young Marion Harland's indifference to her but to become a leader in Richmond social circles—even becoming secretary of the exclusive Mount

Vernon Association—is a testament to her rhetorical skill.

Mowatt is almost invariably referred to by her contemporaries as a "lady." The following description from theater historian Joseph N. Ireland writing in 1866 is typical of descriptions of Mowatt:

> This lady (the daughter of Samuel G. Ogden, of New York, great-granddaughter of Francis Lewis, who signed the Declaration of Independence, and wife of James Mowatt, once well known in the financial circles of the city) had resorted to general literature, dramatic writing, public readings, and finally donned the mantle of Thespis for a livelihood, in all of which employments she was liberally patronized by the very elite of New York society and the widely scattered public of the Union at large. Her American success might have been attributed to the sympathy deeply felt for a countrywoman so fair and unfortunate; but when in after years a career of equal brilliancy was accorded her in the more fastidious theatrical circles of our father-land, it could scarcely be doubted as the result of appreciated skill and merit. Delicacy was her most marked characteristic.[9]

Ireland approvingly notes Mowatt's social connections though means of birth, marriage and association alongside his record of her career triumphs.

Compare the wording of this description to Ireland's equally laudatory paragraph on actress Charlotte Cushman:

> It is generally conceded that Miss Cushman occupies the highest position ever awarded an American actress, and she is certainly the most widely known, the most distinguished and popular, if not the

greatest and best of all the native-born daughters of Thespis. She is descended from a genuine Puritan stock, her original ancestor in America, Robert Cushman, having delivered, within a year after landing at Plymouth, the first sermon in this country now extant. Miss Cushman was born at Boston, in 1815, and the death of her father, a merchant of that city, left her mother with five children, dependent on their own exertions for subsistence. Our heroine was the eldest...[10]

Despite Cushman's Puritan heritage, never in the five pages he spends summarizing her career did Ireland refer to her as a lady. Instead he described her character in the following manner:

> She was always a grave, earnest, self-reliant woman, and her indomitable force of character is what has carried her through her difficult path, in spite of physical disadvantages and disheartening discouragements, to the topmost round of triumph. In private life, Miss Cushman is represented to be all that is admirable, estimable, and virtuous in woman.[11]

There are few instances of the word "lady" being attached to the name of any actress before Mowatt in Ireland's multi-volume *Records of the New York Stage*. Ireland and his peers did not bestow the appellation of "lady" lightly even in the case of Charlotte Cushman or other well respected actresses.

Finally, I feel confident in asserting that Mowatt succeeded in her quest for discursive authority without sacrificing her role as lady because of the sort of social circles in which she continued to be accepted despite actions that might have disqualified her as a lady. As I mentioned earlier, Mowatt became the secretary of the Mount Vernon Association. Her wedding was an elaborate society affair, attended by President Franklin Pierce, his cabinet, and several members of Congress and the Virginia Legislature.[12] Among numerous social engagements recorded by Marius Blesi in his "Life and Letters of Anna Cora Mowatt" he mentions that Mrs. John Tyler, wife of the former president, gave a dinner in her honor during Mowatt's stay in Richmond.[13] Hiram Fuller declared of her and her husband William F. Ritchie that there were "few persons in the Republic better qualified to grace a foreign court."[14] In an obituary of Mowatt, J.W.S. Hows states that the Ritchie residence after Anna Cora's arrival became "the focus of all that was refined and cultivated in the society of Richmond."[15] Anna Cora's social peers were seemingly comfortable not only with permitting her into their exclusive enclaves, but acknowledging her as a leader and example of the best qualities of their class.

Tracy C. Davis suggests that when looking at the lives of female artists all theater historians should ask, "How does the ideology of the dominant culture affect the social status of women performers?" In answer, I say that as much as Mowatt strived to write her life, her life was also written by her society. Not only as a performer but as a female author of non-fiction, fiction, plays, and poetry, Mowatt, like other creative women of the Victorian era, by "engaging in insecure, itinerant, and bohemian occupations," to use Davis' words, "pushed beyond the traditional consciousness of home-centered females and engaged in an active struggle with the ideology of the dominant (masculine) culture."[16] While official religious and legal institutions of patriarchal culture did not formally preclude women from engaging in such pursuits, the cultural context determined the social meaning of creative women's public lives and generically fixed all aspects of their status in the community at large without respect to actual personal conduct.[17]

Was Anna Cora Mowatt's quest for discursive authority subversive? My answer must be no. She did not single-handedly bring about radical change in her society. In my opinion, no individual can single-handedly bring about change in any society. I believe social change is the result of group, not individual action. An individual may point out that change is needed and desirable, but participants must co-operate in order to bring about change.

Was Mowatt's quest for discursive authority an oppositional practice? Marie Maclean has crystallized De Certeau's description of oppositional practice into the following definition:

> It is not a revolutionary movement, it is not aimed at overthrowing society and does not operate from a position of strength. Rather it contests, affirms solidarity, gains victories within a society, operating from a position of weakness.[18]

Oppositional practices therefore are not ones aimed at overthrowing a society in a sudden convulsive movement, but ones that bring about radical change slowly by reshaping society bit by bit. Anna Cora Mowatt was not interested in overthrowing her society. It was always her desire to be seen as a lady—a member of the most powerful class in her society. When she spoke as a lady, she did not speak from a position of weakness. However I still wish to suggest that Mowatt's act of creating discursive authority—not the woman herself—can be seen as oppositional. Operating from a combination of strengths and weaknesses, Mowatt's act of creating discursive authority for herself was one of many acts by many women that helped to broaden the definition of the role of lady. The loosening of restrictions on the role of lady, in turn, was in my opinion, one of many effects brought about by many people that eventually changed the role of women in American society.

Hannah Arendt once wrote, "If we do not know our history, we are condemned to live it as though it were our private fate." I was motivated to write about Anna Cora Mowatt Ritchie by the calls of feminists for a more comprehensive "memory bank" of female role models. Women, such as Anna Cora Mowatt Ritchie, whose actions worked against the prevailing attitudes of her society while still functioning within most of the expectations of that society, are as important to those who study social change as are the actions of those who separated themselves from the mainstream. Popular culture, then as today, is a potent arena for debate on cultural policy.

Mowatt's present day anonymity is, I think, a function of the widespread discomfort with the sort of tactics she utilized to stay in harmony with her socio-cultural setting. We who have had our consciousness raised by feminist thought are as uneasy with her uncomplaining or apologetic acceptance of many forms of patriarchal condescension or limitations aimed at her simply because she was a woman as modern African-Americans are with the "comic darky" performances of the nineteenth and early twentieth century. Today, we are not yet enough removed from the struggle for equality for women to dismiss, let alone find humorous, the fashionable compromises Mowatt made in order to succeed in making her voice heard by her peers.

However we must not let our current sensibilities diminish our ability to appreciate the accomplishments of those who lived in less fortunate times. Mowatt's flutterings and faintings should not blind us to the fact that she was an independent career-oriented woman who fought for and won discursive authority in a situation where the odds were strongly against her being able to do so. Anna Cora Mowatt presented herself to the public in the culturally questionable roles of actress and lady author and yet was still generally acclaimed a lady. Mowatt was a woman of her times who must be understood within the context of those times; however, the narrative and rhetorical strategies she used to combat the prejudices of her contemporaries are not hopelessly dated and obsolete techniques of resistance. Even if Anna Cora Mowatt's creative products are forgotten relics of another time, her multifaceted quest for an authoritative voice should not be.

NOTES

Chapter 1
Fashioned Lady:
The Life and Many Careers of Anna Cora Mowatt

1. William Ogden Wheeler, <u>The Ogden Family in America: Elizabethtown Branch</u> (Philadelphia: J.B. Lippincott, 1907) 154.
2. Eric Wollencott Barnes, <u>The Life and Theater of Anna Cora Mowatt</u> (London: Secker and Warburg, 1954) 14.
3. Mary Howitt, "Memoirs of Anna Cora Mowatt," <u>Howitt's Journal</u> 3 (March 5, 1848): 146.
4. Anna Cora Mowatt, <u>Autobiography of an Actress</u> (Boston: Ticknor, Reed and Fields, 1853) 25.
5. Mowatt, <u>Autobiography</u>, 55.
6. Stanley J. Kuntz and Howard Haycraft, eds. <u>American Authors 1600-1900: A Biographical Dictionary of American Literature </u>(New York: H.W. Wilson Co. 1938) 549.
7.   Mowatt, <u>Autobiography</u>, 63.
8. Anna Cora Mowatt, <u>Pelayo; or, The Cavern of Covandonga, A Romance by Isabel</u> (New York: Harper and Brothers, 1836) xii.
9. Anna Cora Mowatt, <u>Reviewers Reviewed: A Satire by the Author of Pelayo</u> (New York: Printed by the author, 1837) 42-43.
10. A variety of reviews are quoted in Blesi, 22-36.
11. Mowatt, <u>Autobiography</u>, 110.
12. Park Benjamin, editorial, <u>New World</u>, vol. II, no. 17 (April 12, 1841) 264.
13. Anna Cora Mowatt, <u>The Fortune Hunter: A Novel of New York Society</u> (Philadelphia: T.B. Peterson, 1844) 12.
14. Anna Cora Mowatt <u>Evelyn; or, A Heart Unmasked. A Tale of Domestic Life</u>, vol. 2 (Philadelphia: G.B. Zieber, 1845) 6.
15. Mowatt, <u>Autobiography</u>, 115.

16.   Edgar Allan Poe, "Anna Cora Mowatt," The Complete
        Works of Edgar Allan Poe. ed. J.A. Harrison, vol. 12
        (New York: Gordian Press, 1986) 464.
17.   Mowatt, Autobiography, 152.
18.   Epes Sargent, letter to H.P. Whipple, January 18, 1848,
        Harvard University Library, Theater Collection.
19.   Sargent 222.
20.   Mowatt, Autobiography, 169.
21.   Mowatt, Autobiography, 202.
22.   Anna Cora Mowatt, Fashion; or, Life in New York. A
        Comedy in Five Acts (New York: S. French, 1849) 6.
23.   Edgar Allan Poe, Writings in the Broadway Journal:
        Nonfictional Prose (New York: Gordian Press, 1986)
        65.
24.   Poe, "Anna Cora Mowatt," 464.
25.   Marius Blesi, "The Life and Letters of Anna Cora
        Mowatt," diss., U of Virginia, 1938, 329.
26.   Anna Cora Mowatt Ritchie, Mimic Life; or, Before and
        Behind the Curtain: A Series of Narratives (Boston:
        Ticknor and Fields, 1856) 143-144.
27.   Anna Cora Mowatt Ritchie, Twin Roses; a Narrative
        (Boston: Ticknor and Fields, 1857) 173-174.
28.   Barnes 395.
29.   Robert Bonner, editorial, Ledger, April 13, 1861, 1.
30.   Patti P. Gillespie, "Anna Cora Ogden Mowatt Ritchie's
        Fairy Fingers: From Eugene Scribe's?" Text and
        Performance Quarterly 1 (1989) 125.
31.   Gillespie 126.
32.   Epes Sargent, The Scientific Basis of Spiritualism
        (Boston: Colby and Rich, 1881) 224.

Chapter 2
A Radiantly Beautiful Smile:
A Brief History of Anna Cora Mowatt

33.   William Ogden Wheeler, The Ogden Family in
        America: Elizabethtown Branch (Philadelphia: J.B.
        Lippincott, 1907) 154.
34.   Eric Wollencott Barnes, The Life and Theater of Anna

Cora Mowatt (London: Secker and Warburg, 1954) 14.

35. Mary Howitt, "Memoirs of Anna Cora Mowatt,"
Howitt's Journal 3 (March 5, 1848): 146.

36. Anna Cora Mowatt, Autobiography of an Actress
(Boston: Ticknor, Reed and Fields, 1853) 25.

37. Mowatt, Autobiography, 55.

38. Stanley J. Kuntz and Howard Haycraft, eds. American
Authors 1600-1900: A Biographical Dictionary of
American Literature (New York: H.W. Wilson Co.
1938) 549.

39. Mowatt, Autobiography, 63.

40. Anna Cora Mowatt, Pelayo; or, The Cavern of
Covandonga, A Romance by Isabel (New York:
Harper and Brothers, 1836) xii.

41. Anna Cora Mowatt, Reviewers Reviewed: A Satire by
the Author of Pelayo (New York: Printed by the
author, 1837) 42-43.

42. A variety of reviews are quoted in Blesi, 22-36.

43. Mowatt, Autobiography, 110.

44. Park Benjamin, editorial, New World, vol. II, no. 17
(April 12, 1841) 264.

45. Anna Cora Mowatt, The Fortune Hunter: A Novel of
New York Society (Philadelphia: T.B. Peterson, 1844)
12.

46. Anna Cora Mowatt Evelyn; or, A Heart Unmasked. A
Tale of Domestic Life, vol. 2 (Philadelphia: G.B.
Zieber, 1845) 6.

47. Mowatt, Autobiography, 115.

48. Edgar Allan Poe, "Anna Cora Mowatt," The Complete
Works of Edgar Allan Poe. ed. J.A. Harrison, vol. 12
(New York: Gordian Press, 1986) 464.

49. Mowatt, Autobiography, 152.

50. Epes Sargent, letter to H.P. Whipple, January 18, 1848,
Harvard University Library, Theater Collection.

51. Sargent 222.

52. Mowatt, Autobiography, 169.

53. Mowatt, Autobiography, 202.

54. Anna Cora Mowatt, Fashion; or, Life in New York. A
Comedy in Five Acts (New York: S. French, 1849) 6.

55.   Edgar Allan Poe, <u>Writings in the Broadway Journal: Nonfictional Prose</u> (New York: Gordian Press, 1986) 65.

56.   Poe, "Anna Cora Mowatt," 464.

57.   Marius Blesi, "The Life and Letters of Anna Cora Mowatt," diss., U of Virginia, 1938, 329.

58.   Anna Cora Mowatt Ritchie, <u>Mimic Life; or, Before and Behind the Curtain: A Series of Narratives</u> (Boston: Ticknor and Fields, 1856) 143-144.

59.   Anna Cora Mowatt Ritchie, <u>Twin Roses; a Narrative</u> (Boston: Ticknor and Fields, 1857) 173-174.

60.   Barnes 395.

61.   Robert Bonner, editorial, Ledger, April 13, 1861, 1.

62.   Patti P. Gillespie, "Anna Cora Ogden Mowatt Ritchie's Fairy Fingers: From Eugene Scribe's?" <u>Text and Performance Quarterly</u> 1 (1989) 125.

63.   Gillespie 126.

64.   Epes Sargent, <u>The Scientific Basis of Spiritualism</u> (Boston: Colby and Rich, 1881) 224.

Chapter 3
Fashioning The Charm:
The Rhetoric of Anna Cora Mowatt's Autobiography

1.   William Pleater Davidge, *Footlight Flashes* (New York: American News Co., 1866) 2.

2.   Avrom Fleishman, "Personal Myth: Three Victorian Autobiographers," *Interpreting the Theatrical Past: Essays in the Historiography of Performance*, eds. Thomas Postlewait and Bruce A. McConachie (Iowa City: University of Iowa Press, 1989) 217.

3.   George P. Landow, *Approaches to Victorian Autobiography* (Athens, OH: Ohio University Press, 1979) xiii.

4.   All figures quoted from Dr. Martin Blesi's "The Life and Letters of Anna Cora Mowatt," diss., U. of Virginia, 1938, 301.

5.   Caroline Ticknor, *Hawthorne and His Publisher* (Boston: Houghton Mifflin, 1913) 125.

6.   Susan Sniader Lanser, *Fictions of Authority: Women Writers and Narrative Voice* (Ithaca: Cornell University Press, 1992) 6.

7.   Lanser 4.

8.   David Goldknopf, "The Confessional Increment: A New Look at the I-Narrator," *JAAC* 28 (Fall, 1969): 13-21. A slightly revised version appears in The Life of the Novel (Chicago: University of Chicago Press, 1972), 25-41.

9.   Harriet Martineau *Society in America*, ed. Seymour Lipset (New Brunswick: Transaction Books, 1962) 231.

10.   Mrs. E. Oakes Smith, *Woman and Her Needs* (New York, 1851) 82.

11.   Mrs. M.O.W. Oliphant, introduction, *The Autobiography and Letters of Mrs. M.O.W. Oliphant* (n.p.: Leicester University Press, 1974) 14.

12.   Susan Sniader Lanser, *The Narrative Act: Point of View in Prose Fiction* (Princeton, N.J: Princeton University Press, 1981) 23.

13.   Quoted in Kenneth Graham's *English Criticism of the Novel 1865-1900* (Oxford: Clarendon Press, 1965) 129.

14.   Anna Cora Mowatt, *Autobiography of an Actress* (Boston: Ticknor, Reed, and Fields, 1853) 164.

15.   Patricia M. Spacks, *The Female Imagination* (New York: Knopf, 1975) 218.

16.   Thomas Postlewait, "Autobiography and Theater History," *Interpreting the Theatrical Past: Essays in the Historiography of Performance*, eds. Thomas Postlewait and Bruce A. McConachie (Iowa City: University of Iowa Press, 1989) 252.

17.   Postlewait 251.

18.   Mowatt 3.

19.   Mowatt 448.

20.   Mowatt 428-9.

21.   Postlewait 259.

22.   Mowatt 3-4.

23.   Mowatt 426-427.

24.   Mowatt 262.

25.   Mowatt 428.
26.   Mowatt 433.
27.   Mowatt 37-38.
28.   Mowatt 39.
29.   Linda H. Peterson, "Biblical Typology and the Self-Portrait of the Poet in Robert Browning," *Approaches to Victorian Autobiography*, ed. George P. Landow (Athens, Ohio: Ohio University Press, 1979) 236.
30.   Carolyn G. Heilbrun, *Writing a Woman's Life* (New York: W.W. Norton and Co., 1988) 52.
31.   Heilbrun 53.
32.   Gerald Prince, *Dictionary of Narratology* (Lincoln, Nebraska: University of Nebraska Press, 1989) 53.
33.   Mowatt 39.
34.   Mowatt 327.
35.   Mowatt 327.
36.   Mowatt 329-330.
37.   Mowatt 331.
38.   Marie MacLean, *Narrative as Performance: The Baudelariean Experiment* (New York: Routledge, 1988) 12.
39.   Mowatt 38.
40.   This material appears in Daniel Gerould's "Russian Formalist Theories of Melodrama," *Journal of American Culture 1* (Spring, 1978): 154-62.
41.   Mowatt 142.
42.   Gerould 156.
43.   David Grimstead, *Melodrama Unveiled: American Theater and Culture 1800-1850* (Chicago: University of Chicago Press, 1968) 173.
44.   Grimstead 174.
45.   Grimstead 177.
46.   Mowatt 216.
47.   Mowatt 215.
48.   Quoted in *Littel's Living Age* Vol. 41, (April, 1854): 33-35.
49.   Personal letter, The Huntington Library of California, Fields Collection, A.L.S. Anna Cora Mowatt to James T. Fields, Sept. 21, 1853.

50.   Living Age, 35.

51.   *The Home Journal* (Jan. 14, 1854) N. pag.

52.   *Harper's Magazine*, Vol. VIII (February, 1854): 427.

53.   *Putnam's Magazine*, Vol. III (February, 1854): 220-21.

54.   Alexander Woollcott, (no title), *New York Times* (January 28, 1917) N.

Chapter 4
Seductions of the Half-Seen World:
The Defense of the Created Self in Anna Cora Mowatt's Fiction

1.   Michel Foucault, "We `Other Victorians'," *The Foucault Reader*, ed. Paul Rabinow (New York: Pantheon Books, 1984) 292.

2.   John Elsom, *Erotic Theater* (New York: Taplinger, 1974), 21.

3.   Elsom 22.

4.   Elsom 22.

5.   Elsom 22.

6.   Tracy C. Davis, "The Actress in Victorian Pornography," Theater Journal (1989): 940.

7.   Davis 296.

8.   Peter Fryer, ed., Forbidden Books of the Victorians (London: The Odyssey Press, 1970) 80.

9.   Quoted in Thomas Postlewait, "Autobiography and Theater History," Interpreting the Theatrical Past, eds. Thomas Postlewait and Bruce A. McConachie (Iowa City: University of Iowa Press, 1989) 265.

10.   Lucy Barton, Historic Costume for the Stage (Boston: Walter H. Baker Co., 1935) 461.

11.   Davis 294.

12.   Davis 297.

13.   Anna Cora Mowatt Ritchie, Mimic Life (Boston: Ticknor, Reed, and Fields, 1856) 5.

14.   Anna Cora Mowatt, Autobiography of an Actress (Boston: Ticknor, Reed, and Fields, 1853) 318.

15.   Ritchie, Mimic Life, 21.

16.   Ritchie, Mimic Life, 19-20.

17. Ritchie, Mimic Life, 32-33.
18. Ritchie, Mimic Life, 203.
19. Ritchie, Mimic Life, 242.
20. Ritchie, Mimic Life, 243-244.
21. Ritchie, Mimic Life, 246-247.
22. Ritchie, Mimic Life, 324.
23. Ritchie, Mimic Life, 323.
24. Ritchie, Mimic Life, 323.
25. Ritchie, Mimic Life, 191.
26. Ritchie, Mimic Life, 195.
27. William Shakespeare, "The Tragedy of Romeo and Juliet" Act IV, scene v, as quoted by Ritchie, Mimic Life, 195.
28. Ritchie, Mimic Life, 284.
29. Ritchie, Mimic Life, 314.
30. Ritchie, Mimic Life, 402-404.
31. Ritchie, Mimic Life, 405.
32. Michael Wheeler, Death and the Future Life in Victorian Literature (New York: Cambridge University Press, 1990) 83.
33. Elsom 24.
34. Ritchie, Mimic Life, 279.
35. Ritchie, Mimic Life, 27.
36. Ritchie, Mimic Life, 184.
37. Nina Auerbach, Private Theatricals (Cambridge, MA: Harvard University Press, 1990) 23.
38. Wheeler 90.
39. Auerbach 25.
40. Steven Marcus, The Other Victorians (London: Weidenfeld and Nicolson, 1964) 280.

Chapter 5
Fear, Loathing and Fashion:
Self-Creation in Anna Cora Mowatt's Drama

1. For discussion of revivals of *Fashion* see Arthur Hobson Quinn, *A History of the American Drama: From the Beginning to the Civil War* (New York: Appleton-Century-Crofts, Inc., 1951) 309-310;

Margaret G. Mayorga, *A Short History of the American Drama* (New York: Dodd, Mead & Co., 1932) 145-147; Montrose J. Moses, *The American Dramatist* (Boston: Little, Brown and Co. 1925) 102-106 and Marius Blesi, "The Life and Letters of Anna Cora Mowatt," diss., U of Virginia, 1938, 170-174.

2. Arthur Hobson Quinn, *A History of the American Drama: From the Beginning to the Civil War* (New York: Appleton-Century-Crofts, Inc., 1951) 312.

3. Edgar Allan Poe, *Writings in The Broadway Journal: Nonfictional Prose*, ed. Burton R. Pollin (New York: Gordian Press, 1986) 77.

4. Poe 77.

5. Park Benjamin, editorial, *New World* June 13, 1840.

6. Anna Cora Mowatt, *Autobiography of an Actress* (Boston: Ticknor, Reed and Fields, 1854) 203.

7. Mowatt, *Autobiography*, 202-3.

8. Mowatt, *Autobiography*, 203.

9. Anna Cora Mowatt to James O. Sargent, April 13, 1847, Harvard University Library Theater Collection, A.L.S.

10. Marius Blesi, "The Life and Letters of Anna Cora Mowatt," diss., U of Virginia, 1938, 148.

11. Blesi 143.

12. John F. Kasson, *Rudeness and Civility: Manners in Nineteenth-Century Urban America* (New York: Hill and Wang, 1990) 223.

13. Blesi 149.

14. Mowatt, *Autobiography*, 207-8.

15. *Spirit of the Times*, March 15, 1845.

16. Anna Cora Mowatt to Edgar Allan Poe, the Griswold Collection, quoted by J.A. Harrison in Life and Letters of Edgar Allan Poe, vol. II, pp. 207-8.

17. *Spirit of the Times*, March 29, 1845.

18. *Spirit of the Times*, April 5, 1845.

19. John William Stanhope Hows, review, *New York Albion*, March 29, 1845.

20. *Evening Post*, March 25, 1845.

21. *New York Herald*, March 26, 1845.

22. Edgar Allan Poe, *Writings in The Broadway Journal:*

Nonfictional Prose, ed. Burton R. Pollin (New York: Gordian Press, 1986) 67.

23.   Poe 68.

24.   Poe 39.

25.   Anna Cora Mowatt, *Fashion: Life in New York, a Comedy in Five Acts* (New York: Samuel French, 1854) 39.

26.   C. Willet Cunnington's "The Sentimental '40's," *Feminine Attitudes in the 19th Century* (London: William Heinemann, 1935) 104.

27.   Mowatt, *Fashion*, 27.

28.   Washington Irving, *Letters of Jonathan Oldstyle*. p. 12.

29.   For further discussion of the causes and implications of the Astor Place Riot see John F. Kasson's *Rudeness and Civility: Manners in Nineteenth-Century Urban America* (New York: Hill and Wang, 1990) 222-227 and Lawrence W. Levine's *Highbrow/Lowbrow: The Emergence of Cultural Hierarchy in America* (Cambridge, Massachusetts: Harvard University Press, 1988) 63-65.

30.   Karen Halttunen, *Confidence Men and Painted Women: A Study of Middle-class Culture in America* (New Haven: Yale University Press, 1982) 5.

31.   Mowatt, *Fashion*, 24.

32.   Mowatt, *Fashion*, 17-18.

33.   Mowatt, *Fashion*, 20.

34.   Kasson 103.

35.   Kasson 104.

36.   Isabella Bird, *The Englishwoman in America* (London: John Murray, 1856) 368.

37.   [James Dabney McCabe], *The Secrets of the Great City: A Work Descriptive of the Virtues and the Vices, the Mysteries, Miseries and Crimes of New York City* (Philadelphia: Jones Brothers, 1868) 15-16.

38.   Eliza Ware Farrar, *The Young Lady's Friend* (n.p.: 1837) 102.

39.   Farrar 102.

40.   Kasson 121.

41.   Mowatt, *Fashion*, ii.

42. Halttunen 144.

43. Halttunen 156.

44. Halttunen 155.

45. Mowatt, *Fashion*, 51.

46. Arthur M. Schlesinger, Jr. *The Age of Jackson*, (Boston: Little, Brown, and Co., 1950) 51.

47. Martin Van Buren, *Autobiography,* ed. J.C. Fitzpatrick, (American Historical Association, Annual Report for the Year 1918, Vol.II: Washington, D.C., 1920) 466-471.

48. Harriet Martineau, *Retrospect of Western Travel,* Vol. I (London, 1838) 243-44.

49. John Quincy Adams, *Memoirs,* ed. C.F. Adams (Philadelphia, 1877) 64.

50. Mowatt, *Fashion*, 22.

51. Ralph Waldo Emerson, *Selected Essays, Lectures and Poems of Ralph Waldo Emerson*, ed. R.E.Spiller (New York: Pocket Books, 1965) 317-321.

52. Diary of Philip Hone, Vol II, 600-601, quoted in Lawrence W. Levine's *Highbrow/Lowbrow: The Emergence of Cultural Hierarchy in America* Cambridge, Massachusetts: Harvard University Press, 1988) 174.

53. Mowatt, *Fashion*, 18.

54. Quoted in Robert V. Remini's *The Jacksonian Era* (Arlington Heights, Illinois: Harlan Davidson, Inc. 1989) 109.

55. Hamilton Luther, Memoirs, *Speeches and Writings of Robert Rantoul, Jr.* (Boston, 1854) 687.

56. Mowatt, Fashion, 17.

57. Susan Sniader Lanser, *The Narrative Act: Point of View in Prose Fiction* (Princeton, New Jersey: Princeton University Press, 1981) 89.

Chapter 6
Exploiting the Medium:
Anna Cora Mowatt's Creation of Self Through Performance

1.   Robert C. Fuller, *Mesmerism and the American Cure of Souls* (Philadelphia: University of Pennsylvannia Press, 1982) xi.
2.   Fuller 183.
3.   Slater Brown, *Heyday of Spiritualism* (New York: Hawthorne Books, Inc. 1970) 2.
4.   Gentleman of Philadelphia, *The Philosophy of Animal Magnetism* ed. Joseph Jackson (Philadelphia: Patterson and White, 1928) 37. Jackson attributes this work to Edgar Allan Poe on largely circumstantial evidence. However, the text is not, in my opinion, in Poe's style and Poe was not the only gentleman in Philadelphia interested in mesmerism at the time of the pamphlet's publication. Scholars on Poe do not generally recognize this booklet as the author's work.
5.   Gentleman 45.
6.   Gentleman 102.
7.   Gentleman 112.
8.   Nathaniel Hawthorne, *The Blithedale Romance* eds. Seymour Gross and Rosalie Murphy (New York: W.W. Norton, 1978) 183.
9.   Hawthorne 182-183.
10.   Hawthorne 185.
11.   Edgar Allan Poe, "Mesmeric Revelation," *The Complete Poems and Stories of Edgar Allan Poe*, vol.2, eds. Arthur Hobson Quinn and Edward H. O'Neill (New York: Alfred A. Knopf, 1964) 543.
12.   Poe, "Mesmeric Revelation," 543.
13.   Bertrand, *Traite du Somnambulisme* (Paris: Dentu, 1823) 12.
14.   See, for example, T.R. Sarbin and W.C. Coe *Hypnotic Behavior: The Psychology of Influence Communication* (New York: Holt, 1972); N.P. Spanos "A Social Psychological Approach to Hypnotic Behavior," *Integrations of Clinical and Social Psychology* eds. G. Wear and H. L. Mirels (New York: Oxford University Press, 1982); N.P. Spanos "Hypnotic Behavior: A Social Psychological Interpretation of Amnesia, Analgesia, and 'Trance Logic'" *The Behavioral and*

Brain Sciences, 9, 1986, 449-502; G.F. Wagstaff *Hypnosis, Compliance and Belief* (Brighton: Harvester Press, 1981); and G.F. Wagstaff "Hypnosis as Compliance and Belief: A Socio-Cognitive View," What is Hypnosis? ed. P.L.N. Naish (Milton Keynes: Open University Press, 1986).

15. Graham F. Wagstaff "Suggestibility: A Social Psychological Approach," *Human Suggestibility: Advances in Theory, Research, and Application* ed. John F. Schumaker . (New York: Routledge, 1991) 136.

16. See J.R. Hilgard *Personality and Hypnosis: A Study of Imaginative Involvement* (Chicago: University of Chicago Press: 1970); S.J. Lynn and J.W. Rhue "The Fantasy Prone Person: Hypnosis, Imagination, and Creativity," *Journal of Personality and Social Psychology*, 51, 1986, 404-08; S.J. Lynn and J.W. Rhue "Fantasy Proneness, Hypnotizability, and Absorption—A Reexamination," *The International Journal of Clinical Experimental Hypnosis*, 37, 100-06; S.J. Lynn and J.W. Rhue "Hypnosis and Beyond: Research on the Fantasy Prone Person," *Hypnos, Swedish Journal of Hypnosis in Psychotherapy and Psychosomatic Medicine*, 16, 1989, 175-87; and S.C. Wilson, and T.X. Barber "The Fantasy-Prone Personality: Implications for Understanding Imagery, Hypnosis, and Parapsychological Phenomena," *Imagery: Current Theory, Research, and Application* ed. A.A. Sheikh (New York: Wiley, 1983) 340-87.

17. Edgar Allan Poe, "Anna Cora Mowatt," *The Complete Works of Edgar Allan Poe*, ed. J.A. Harrison, vol. 12 (New York: Gordian Press, 1986) 426.

18. Epes Sargent, *The Scientific Basis of Spiritualism*, (Boston: Colby and Rich, 1881) 218.

19. Sargent 216.

20. Edgar Allan Poe, "Epes Sargent," *The Complete Works of Edgar Allan Poe*. ed. J.A. Harrison, vol. 12 (New York: Gordian Press, 1986) 527.

21. Sargent 218.

22.   Sargent 368.
23.   Sargent 217.
24.   Sargent 219.
25.   Sargent 220.
26.   Poe, "Epes Sargent," 528.
27.   Sargent 223.
28.   Ruth Brandon, *The Spiritualists* (London: Weidenfeld
        and Nicolson, 1983) 88.
29.   Sargent 213.
30.   Marius Blesi, "The Life and Letters of Anna Cora
        Mowatt" diss., U of Virginia, 1938, 86.
31.   Sargent 216.
32.   Mary Howitt, "Memoirs of Anna Cora Mowatt,"
        Howitt's Journal 3 (March 5, 1848) 167.
33.   Brown 51.
34.   Brown 44.
35.   Sargent 368.
36.   Anna Cora Mowatt, *Autobiography of an Actress*
        (Boston: Ticknor, Reed, and Fields, 1853) 169.
37.   Mowatt 182.
38.   Emanuel Swedenborg, "Divine Providence," A
        Compendium of the Theological Writings of Emanuel
        Swedenborg, ed. Samuel M. Warren (New York:
        Swedenborg Foundation, 1974) 485.
39.   Sargent 363.
40.   Emanuel Swedenborg "Marriage," *A Compendium of
        the Theological Writings of Emanuel Swedenborg*, ed.
        Samuel M. Warren (New York: Swedenborg
        Foundation, 1974) 473.
41.   Mowatt 161.
42.   Mowatt 167.

Chapter 7
A Fairy's Dream:
Self-Creation in the Poetry of Anna Cora Mowatt

1.   Marius Blesi, "The Life and Letters of Anna Cora
        Mowatt" diss.,U of Virginia, 1938, 96.
2.   Edgar Allan Poe, "Anna Cora Mowatt," *The Complete*

Works of Edgar Allan Poe, ed. J.A. Harrison, vol. 12 (New York: Gordian Press, 1986) 459-460.

3. Rufus Wilmot Griswold, *The Female Poets of America* (Philadelphia: Carey and Hart: 1848) 268.

4. Blesi, 96.

5. Sarah Josepha Hale, editorial, *American Ladies Magazine* VII: 53 (April 1834), 153.

6. Joy Bayless, *Rufus Wilmot Griswold: Poe's Literary Executor* (Nashville, TN: Vanderbilt University Press, 1943) 55-56.

7. Angela Leighton, *Victorian Women Poets: Writing Against the Heart* (Charlottesville: University Press of Virginia, 1992) 10-11.

8. Isabelle Webb Entrikin, *Sarah Josepha Hale and Godey's Lady's Book* (Philadelphia: Lancaster Press, 1946) 121.

9. Entrikin 28-29.

10. Entrikin 55.

11. Sarah Josepha Hale, letter to Carey and Hart, Nov. 19, 1835, Library Company, Ridgeway Branch, Philadelphia.

12. Leighton, 50-51.

13. Leighton 2.

14. Caroline May, *The American Female Poets with Biographical and Critical Notices* (Philadelphia: Linsay and Blackiston, 1848) v.

15. Leighton 2.

16. George Gilfillan, review, *Tait's Edinburgh Magazine*, 14 (1847) 361.

17. Anna Cora Mowatt, *Autobiography of an Actress* (Boston: Ticknor, Reed, and Fields, 1853) 161.

18. Leighton 29.

19. Leighton 29.

20. Griswold 7.

21. Mowatt, *Autobiography*, 31-32.

22. May vi.

23. Anna Cora Mowatt, "My Life," *The Female Poets of America*, ed. Rufus Wilmot Griswold (Philadelphia: Carey and Hart: 1848) 269.

24.   Griswold 7.
25.   Leighton 57.
26.   Anna Cora Mowatt, "Love," *The Female Poets of America*, ed. Rufus Wilmot Griswold (Philadelphia: Carey and Hart: 1848) 269.
27.   Anna Cora Mowatt, "On a Lock of My Mother's Hair," *The Female Poets of America*, ed. Rufus Wilmot Griswold (Philadelphia: Carey and Hart: 1848) 269.

Chapter 8
"And Earth is Fleeting By:"
Reflections on the Legacy of Anna Cora Mowatt

1.   Arthur Hobson Quinn, *A History of the American Drama* (New York: Appelton-Century-Crofts, Inc., 1951) 319.
2.   Laurence Hutton, *Curiosities of the American Stage* (New York: Harper and Brothers, 1891) 64-65.
3.   Anna Cora Mowatt, *Autobiography of an Actress* (Boston: Ticknor, Reed, and Fields, 1853) 157.
4.   For further discussion of similarities in program and publicity design between Mowatt and later female public readers see Bill Jaye Schooley, "Anna Cora Mowatt: Public Reader" thesis, Louisiana State University, 1980, 76-80.
5.   Susan Sniader Lanser, *Fictions of Authority: Women Writers and Narrative Voice* (Cornell University Press: Ithaca, 1992) 24.
6.   Mowatt 142.
7.   Mowatt 142.
8.   Marion Harland, *Marion Harland's Autobiography: The Story of a Long Life* (New York: Harper and Brothers, 1910) 289.
9.   Joseph N. Ireland, *Records of the New York Stage* (1866; New York: Burt Franklin,1968) 438.
10.   Ireland 159.
11.   Ireland 161.
12.   Marius Blesi, "The Life and Letters of Anna Cora Mowatt" diss., U. of Virginia, 1938, 327.

13.   Blesi 330.
14.   Hiram Fuller, *Belle Britain on a Tour* (New York: Derby and Jackson, 1856) 147.
15.   J. W. S. Hows, "Anna Cora Mowatt," *New York Tribune*, Aug. 27, 1870, np.
16.   Tracy C. Davis, "Questions for a Feminist Methodology in Theater History," *Interpreting the Theatrical Past: Essays in the Historiography of Performance*, eds. Thomas Postlewait and Bruce A. McConachie (Iowa City: University of Iowa Press, 1989) 69.
17.   Davis 69.
18.   Marie Maclean, "Oppositional Practices in Women's Traditional Narrative," *New Literary History* Vol.19 (1987-88) 40.

SELECTED BIBLIOGRAPHY

Works on or by Anna Cora Mowatt:

Barnes, Eric Wollencott. *The Lady of Fashion*. New York: Charles Scribner's Sons, 1954.

—-. *The Life and Theater of Anna Cora Mowatt*. London: Secker and Warburg, 1954.

Blesi, Marius. "The Life and Letters of Anna Cora Mowatt." Diss. U of Virginia, 1938.

Butler, Mildred Allen. *Actress in Spite of Herself.* New York: Funk & Wagnalls, 1966.

Freeman, Julia Deane. *Women of the South Distinguished in Literature*. New York: Derby and Jackson, 1861.

Gentile, John S. *Cast of One*. Chicago: University of Illinois Press, 1989.

Gillespie, Patti P. "Anna Cora Ogden Mowatt Ritchie's Fairy Fingers: From Eugene Scribes?" *Text and Performance Quarterly* 2 (1989): 125-134.

Griswold, Rufus W. *The Female Poets of America*. Philadelphia: Carey and Hart, 1849.

Harland, Marian. "Personal Recollections of a Christian Actress." *Our Continent* 1 (March 15, 1882): 73-74.

—-. Marion Harland's Autobiography: *The Story of a Long Life*. New York: Harper and Brothers, 1910.

Howitt, Mary. "Memoir of Anna Cora Mowatt," *Howitt's Journal* 3 (March 4, 1848): 146-49; (March 11, 1848): 167-70; (March 18, 1848): 181-85.

Hutton, Laurence. *Curiosities of the American Stage*. New York: Harper and Brothers, 1891.

Ireland, Joseph Norton. *Records of the New York Stages from 1750-1860*. New York: T.H. Morrell Publishers, 1940.

May, Caroline. *The American Female Poets with Biographical and Critical Notices*. Philadelphia: Linsay and

Blackiston, 1848.

McCarthy, Imogene Jones. "Anna Cora Mowatt and Her Audience." Thesis. U of Maryland, 1952.

Mowatt, Anna Cora. *Autobiography of an Actress*. Boston: Ticknor, Reed, and Fields, 1853.

—-. *Fashion: Life in New York, a Comedy in Five Acts*. New York: Samuel French, 1854.

Murphy, Theresa. "Interpretation in the Dickens Period." *The Quarterly Journal of Speech* 41 (October 1955): 243-49.

Odell, George C.D. *Annals of the New York Stage*. 15 vols. New York: Columbia University Press, 1927-1949.

Poe, Edgar Allan. *Writings in The Broadway Journal: Nonfictional Prose*. Ed. Burton R. Pollin. New York: Gordian Press, 1986.

—-. "Anna Cora Mowatt." *The Complete Works of Edgar Allan Poe*. Ed. J.A. Harrison. New York: Gordian Press, 1986.

—-. "Epes Sargent." *The Complete Works of Edgar Allan Poe*. Ed. J.A. Harrison. New York: Gordian Press, 1986.

Quinn, Arthur Hobson. *A History of the American Drama: From the Beginning to the Civil War*. New York: Appleton-Century-Crofts, Inc., 1951.

Ritchie, Anna Cora Mowatt. *Mimic Life*. Boston: Ticknor, Reed, and Fields, 1856.

Sargent, Epes. *The Modern Standard Drama*. New York: Wm. Taylor and Co., 1846.

—-. *The Scientific Basis of Spiritualism*. Boston: Colby and Rich, 1881.

Schooley, Bill Jaye. "Anna Cora Mowatt: Public Reader." Thesis. Louisiana State University, 1980.

Thompson, David W. "Early Actress-Readers: Mowatt, Kemble, and Cushman." Ed. D.W. Thompson.

Performance of Literature in Historical Perspective.
New York: University Press of America, 1983.

Wheeler, William Ogden. *The Ogden Family in America:
Elizabethtown Branch.* Philadelphia: J.B. Lippincott,
1907.

Wise, John S. "Mrs. Anna Cora Ritchie." *Report of the
Virginia Board of Visitors to Mount Vernon.*
Richmond: J.H. O'Bennon, 1901.

Works on Victorian Theater:

Barrish, Jonas. *The Antitheatrical Prejudice.* Berkeley:
University of California Press, 1981.

Bellinger, Martha Fletcher. *A Short History of the Drama.*
New York: Henry Hold, 1927.

Brown, Thomas A. *History of the American Stage.* New York:
Dick and Fitzgerald, 1870.

Chinoy, Helen Krish, and Linda Walsh Jenkins. *Women in
American Theater.* New York: Theater
Communications Group, 1981.

Clapp, William Warland. *A Record of the Boston Stage.*
Boston: James Monroe and Co., 1853.

Davidge, William Pleater. *Footlight Flashes.* New York:
American News Co., 1866.

Davis, Tracy C. "The Actress in Victorian Pornography."
Theater Journal (1989): 294-310.

Edgett, Edward Francis. *Edward Loomis Davenport.* New
York: The Dunlap Society, 1901.

Elsom, John. *Erotic Theater.* New York: Taplinger, 1974.

Fleishman, Avrom. "Personal Myth: Three Victorian
Autobiographers." *Interpreting the Theatrical Past:
Essays in the Historiography of Performance.* Eds.
Thomas Postlewait and Bruce A. McConachie. Iowa
City: University of Iowa Press, 1989.

Freedley, George A. and John Reeves. *History of The Theater.*

New York: Crown Publishers, 1941.

Gerould, Daniel. "Russian Formalist Theories of Melodrama."
Journal of American Culture 1 (Spring, 1978): 154-62.

Grimstead, David. *Melodrama Unveiled: American Theater
and Culture 1800-1850.* Chicago: University of
Chicago Press, 1968.

Hall, Lillian Arvilla. *Catalogue of Dramatic Portraits in the
Theater Collection of Harvard College Library.*
Cambridge: Harvard University Press, 1932.

Hughes, Glenn. *History of the American Theater 1700-1950.*
New York: Samuel French, 1951.

Kendall, John S. *The Golden Age of the New Orleans Theater.*
Baton Rouge: Louisiana State University Press, 1952.

Ludlow, Noah Miller. *Dramatic Life as I found It.* St. Louis:
G. I. Jones and Co., 1880.

Mayorga, Margret G. *A Short History of the American Drama.*
New York: Dodd, Mead, and Co., 1932.

Moses, Montrose J. *The American Dramatist.* Boston: Little,
Brown and Co., 1945.

Postlewait, Thomas. "Autobiography and Theater History."
Interpreting the Theatrical Past. Eds. Thomas
Postlewait and Bruce A. McConachie. Iowa City:
University of Iowa Press, 1989.

Works on Victorian Culture:

Adams, John Quincy. *Memoirs.* Ed. C.F. Adams. N. p.:
Philadelphia, 1877.

Auerbach, Nina. *Private Theatricals.* Cambridge,
Massachusetts: Harvard University Press, 1990.

Barreca, Regina, ed. *Sex and Death in Victorian Literature.*
Bloomington: Indiana University Press, 1990.

Bayless, Joy. *Rufus Wilmot Griswold: Poe's Literary
Executor.* Nashville: Vanderbilt University Press,
1943.

Bird, Isabella. *The Englishwoman in America.* London: John Murray, 1856.

Bode, Carl, ed. *American Life in the 1840's.* New York: Doubleday, 1967.

Buren, Martin Van. *Autobiography.* Ed. J.C. Fitzpatrick. American Historical Association, Annual Report for the Year 1918, Vol.II: Washington, D.C., 1920.

Buhle, Mari Jo, Gordon, Ann D., and Schrom, Nancy E. *Women in American Society.* Andover, Massachusetts: Warner Modular Publications, 1973.

Cunnington C. Willet. *Feminine Attitudes in the 19th Century.* London: William Heinemann, 1935.

Emerson, Ralph Waldo. *Selected Essays, Lectures and Poems of Ralph Waldo Emerson.* Ed. R.E.Spiller. New York: Pocket Books, 1965.

Entrikin, Isabelle Webb. *Sarah Josepha Hale and Godey's Lady's Book.* Philadelphia: Lancaster Press, 1946.

Farrar, Eliza Ware. *The Young Lady's Friend.* N.p: 1837.

Fryer, Peter, ed. *Forbidden Books of the Victorians.* London: The Odyssey Press, 1970.

Hale, Sarah Josepha. Editorial. *American Ladies Magazine* VII: 53 (April 1834), 153.

—-. *Women's Record: or, Sketches of Distinguished Women from the Creation to A.D. 1850.* New York: Harper, 1853.

Halttunen, Karen. *Confidence Men and Painted Women: A Study of Middle-Class Culture in America.* New Haven: Yale University Press, 1982.

Hellerstein, Erna Olafson, Leslie Parker Hume, and Karen M. Offen, eds. *Victorian Women: A Documentary Account of Women's Lives in Nineteenth Century England, France, and the United States.* Stanford: Stanford University Press, 1981.

Kasson, John F. *Rudeness and Civility: Manners in Nineteenth-Century Urban America*. New York: Hill and Wang, 1990.

Landow, George P. *Approaches to Victorian Autobiography*. Athens, OH: Ohio University Press, 1979.

Leighton, Angela. *Victorian Women Poets: Writing Against the Heart*. Charlottesville: University Press of Virginia, 1992.

Levine, Lawrence W. *Highbrow/Lowbrow: The Emergence of Cultural Hierarchy in America*. Cambridge, Massachusetts: Harvard University Press, 1988.

Luther, Hamilton. *Memoirs, Speeches and Writings of Robert Rantoul, Jr*. Boston, 1854.

Marcus, Steven. *The Other Victorians*. London: Weidenfeld and Nicolson, 1964.

Martineau, Harriet. *Society in America*. Ed. Seymour Lipset. New Brunswick: Transaction Books, 1962.

McCabe, James Dabney. *The Secrets of the Great City: A Work Descriptive of the Virtues and the Vices, the Mysteries, Miseries and Crimes of New York City*. Philadelphia: Jones Brothers, 1868.

Oliphant, Mrs. M.O.W. *The Autobiography and Letters of Mrs. M.O.W. Oliphant*. N.p.: Leicester University Press, 1974.

Peterson, Linda H. "Biblical Typology and the Self-Portrait of the Poet in Robert Browning." *Approaches to Victorian Autobiography*. Ed. George P. Landow. Athens, Ohio: Ohio University Press, 1979.

Remini, Robert V. *The Jacksonian Era*. Arlington Heights, Illinois: Harlan Davidson, Inc. 1989.

Schlesinger, Arthur M. *The Age of Jackson*. Boston: Little, Brown, and Co., 1950.

Smith, E. Oakes. *Woman and Her Needs*. New York: n.p., 1851.

Swedenborg, Emanuel. *A Compendium of the Theological Writings of Emanuel Swedenborg*. Ed. Samuel M. Warren. New York: Swedenborg Foundation, 1974.

Ticknor, Caroline. *Hawthorne and His Publisher*. Boston: Houghton Mifflin, 1913.

Wheeler, Michael. *Death and the Future Life in Victorian Literature and Theology*. New York: Cambridge University Press, 1990.

Wiskell, Milton Joel. "Social Aspects of 19th Century American Elocution." Diss. Louisiana State University, 1948.

Works on Mesmerism and Hypnosis:

Bertrand, A. *Traite du Somnambulisme*. Paris: Dentu, 1823.

Brandon, Ruth. *The Spiritualists*. London: Weidenfeld and Nicolson, 1983.

Brown, Slater. *Heyday of Spiritualism*. New York: Hawthorne Books, Inc. 1970.

Fuller, Robert C. *Mesmerism and the American Cure of Souls*. Philadelphia: University of Pennsylvania Press, 1982.

Gentleman of Philadelphia. *The Philosophy of Animal Magnetism*. Ed. Joseph Jackson. Philadelphia: Patterson and White, 1928.

Hawthorne, Nathaniel. *The Blithedale Romance*. Seymour Gross and Rosalie Murphy, eds. New York: W.W. Norton, 1978.

Hilgard, J.R. *Personality and Hypnosis: A Study of Imaginative Involvement*. Chicago: University of Chicago Press, 1970.

Lynn, S.J. and J.W. Rhue. "Fantasy Proneness, Hypnotizability, and Absorption—A Reexamination." *The International Journal of Clinical Experimental Hypnosis*, 37, 100-06.

—. "Hypnosis and Beyond: Research on the Fantasy Prone

Person." *Hypnos, Swedish Journal of Hypnosis in Psychotherapy and Psychosomatic Medicine*, 16, 1989, 175-87.

—. "The Fantasy Prone Person: Hypnosis, Imagination, and Creativity." *Journal of Personality and Social Psychology*, 51, 1986, 404-08.

Poe, Edgar Allan. "Mesmeric Revelation." *The Complete Poems and Stories of Edgar Allan Poe*. Eds. Arthur Hobson Quinn and Edward H. O'Neill. New York: Alfred A. Knopf, 1964.

Sarbin, T.R. and W.C. Coe. *Hypnotic Behavior: The Psychology of Influence Communication*. New York: Holt, 1972.

Spanos, N.P. "A Social Psychological Approach to Hypnotic Behavior." *Integrations of Clinical and Social Psychology*. Eds. G. Wear and H. L. Mirels. New York: Oxford University Press, 1982.

—. "Hypnotic Behavior: A Social Psychological Interpretation of Amnesia, Analgesia, and 'Trance Logic'." *The Behavioral and Brain Sciences*, 9, 1986, 449-502.

Wagstaff, G.F. "Hypnosis as Compliance and Belief: A Socio-Cognitive View." *What is Hypnosis?* Ed. P.L.N. Naish. Milton Keynes: Open University Press, 1986.

—. *Hypnosis, Compliance and Belief*. Brighton: Harvester Press, 1981.

—. "Suggestibility: A Social Psychological Approach." *Human Suggestibility: Advances in Theory, Research, and Application*. Ed. John F. Schumaker. New York: Routledge, 1991.

Wilson, S.C. and T.X. Barber. "The Fantasy-Prone Personality: Implications for Understanding Imagery, Hypnosis, and Parapsychological Phenomena." *Imagery: Current Theory, Research, and Application*. Ed. A.A. Sheikh. New York: Wiley, 1983.

Works on Discursive Authority:

Certeau, Michel de. *The Practice of Everyday Life*. Berkeley: University of California Press, 1988.

Eakin, Paul John. *Studies in the Art of Self-Invention*. Princeton, New Jersey: Princeton University Press, 1985.

Foucault, Michel. "Of Other Spaces." *Diacritics 16* (Spring 1986): 22-27.

—-. "We 'Other Victorians'." *The Foucault Reader*. Paul Rabinow, ed. New York: Pantheon Books, 1984.

Goldknopf, David. "The Confessional Increment: A New Look at the I-Narrator," *JAAC* 28 (Fall, 1969): 13-21.

Greenblatt, Stephen. *Renaissance Self-Fashioning*. Chicago: The University of Chicago Press, 1985.

Heilbrun, Carolyn G. *Writing a Woman's Life*. New York: W.W. Norton and Co., 1988.

Lanser, Susan Sniader. *Fictions of Authority: Women Writers and Narrative Voice*. Ithaca: Cornell University Press, 1992.

—-. *The Narrative Act: Point of View in Prose Fiction*. Princeton, N.J: Princeton University Press, 1981.

MacLean, Marie. *Narrative as Performance: The Baudelariean Experiment*. New York: Routledge, 1988.

Prince, Gerald. *Dictionary of Narratology*. Lincoln, Nebraska: University of Nebraska Press, 1989.

Rosenwald, George C., and Richard L. Ochberg, eds. *Storied Lives: The Cultural Politics of Understanding*. New Haven: Yale University Press, 1992.

Spacks, Patricia M. *The Female Imagination*. New York: Knopf, 1975.

APPENDIX A

CHRONOLOGY OF THE LIFE OF ANNA CORA MOWATT

1819	March 5	Born in Bordeaux, France
1825		Travels to New York with Parents
1834	October 6	Marries James Mowatt
1841	April	Publication of *Gulzara, or the Persian Slave*
1841	October 28	Appears as a public reader for the first time in Boston
1845	March 24	*Fashion* opens at the Park Theater, New York
1845	June 13	Debuts as an actress at the Park Theater
1846	September	E.L. Davenport joins Mowatt as acting partner
1847	November 1	Davenport and Mowatt sail for England
1851	February 15	James Mowatt dies
1851	July	Anna Cora Mowatt returns to America
1853	December	Publishes *Autobiography of an Actress*
1853	June 3	Retires from the stage
1853	June 7	Marries William Foushee Ritchie
1855		Writes *Mimic Life*
1857		Writes *Twin Roses*

1860	April 5	Samuel G. Ogden (Mowatt's father) dies
1860	August 20	Sails for Europe (leaving Ritchie)
1861		Writes *The Mute Singer*
1861-63		Lives in Paris, France
1863-65		Lives in Florence, Italy
1865		Writes *Fairy Fingers*
1865-70		Lives in England
1870	July 21	Dies in Twickenham, England

APPENDIX B

LISTING OF SIGNIFICANT EVENTS OCCURRING DURING THE LIFETIME OF ANNA CORA MOWATT

1803		F.A. Winsor invents gas-lighting
1812		Siege of Moscow lifted
1812		The Battle of 1812 between U.S. and England
1815		Napoleon defeated at Waterloo
1815	December	First successful professional theater group in the American West established in Frankfort, KY
1816	November 25	Introduction of gas lighting into Chestnut theater
1818		Appearance of first English-speaking company in New Orleans under Noah Ludlow.
1820		The Missouri Compromise
1820	April 2	Chestnut Street Theater burns in Philadelphia
	May 24	Park Theater burns in New York
	November 27	Debut of Edwin Forrest, age 16
1821	September	Rebuilt Park Theater Reopens
		Debut of Junius Brutus Booth in Richmond
1822		Opening of rebuilt Chestnut Theater
1823		The Monroe Doctrine
1824	January 1	Opening of James Caldwell's Camp Theater in New Orleans.

1826	October 23	Opening of the 3,000 seat Bowery Theater, New York.
1825		Erie Canal opens
1827		Tremont Street Theater opens in Boston
		Caldwell opens a theater in St. Louis
1830		Riots accompany production of Victor Hugo's *Hernani* in Paris.
		The "Tom Thumb", America's first commercial steam locomotive, operates in Baltimore
1831		William Lloyd Garrison founds "The Liberator"
1832		South Carolina threatens secession over "Tariff of Abominations"
1833		St. Charles Theater opens in New Orleans
1834		Cyrus McCormick patents the reaper
1835		Oberlin College becomes first men's college to admit women
1837		Samuel F. B. Morse demonstrates first successful telegraph in U.S.
1841	October	*London Assurance*, by Boucicault opens at Park.
1844		Taglioni dances *Giselle*
1845	March 24	*Fashion*, by Mowatt debuts
1846		England cedes southern part of

		Oregon Country to U.S.
1847		J.B. Rice constructs first theater in Chicago
1848		"Year of Revolutions" in Europe
		Gold Rush starts in California
		U.S. victory in Mexican American War
		New York becomes the first state to allow married women to own real estate
		Women's Rights Convention held in Seneca Falls, N.Y.
1849	May 10	Astor Place Riot, New York.
	September 10	Debut of Edwin Booth in Boston
	October 18	First performance of a professional play in California (*The Bandit Chief* at Eagle Theater, Sacramento)
1850		Compromise of 1850 temporarily ends national crisis over slavery question
1852	March 20	Publication of *Uncle Tom's Cabin* in book form.
1853		The Gadsden Purchase
1853	July 18	Opening of *Uncle Tom's Cabin* at Purdy's, New York.
1854		Opening of the New Boston Theater
		Passage of Kansas-Nebraska Act
1855		Dion Boucicault appears in *Grimaldi* in Cincinnati

1856	August 18	First American copyright law to give author sole right to print, publish, act, perform, and present own plays
1859		John Brown and followers seize federal arsenal at Harpers Ferry, VA
1861		Brigham Young erects Salt Lake Theater
		American Civil War begins
1863		The Emancipation Proclamation
1865		Civil War ends
1865		John Wilkes Booth assassinates President Lincoln, Ford's Theater, Washington.
1867		U.S. buys Alaska from Russia

APPENDIX C

LISTING OF SELECTED AMERICAN AND EUROPEAN CONTEMPORARIES OF ANNA CORA MOWATT IN LITERATURE AND DRAMATIC ARTS

(1736-1826) Francois-Joseph Talma

(1749-1832) Johann Wolfgang Goethe

(1755-1831) Sarah Siddons

(1757-1823) John Philip Kemble

(1766-1817) Madame de Stael

(1770-1850) William Wordsworth

(1771-1832) Sir Walter Scott

(1772-1834) Samuel Taylor Coleridge

(1783-1859) Washington Irving

(1787-1823) Edmond Kean

(1788-1824) Lord Byron

(1788-1879) Sarah Josepha Hale

(1789-1851) James Fennimore Cooper

(1790-1861) James M. Vanderhoff

(1791-1832) Percy Bysshe Shelley

(1792-1822) Sheridan Knowles

(1793-1835) Felicia Hemans

(1793-1873) William Charles MacReady

(1794-1878) William Cullen Bryant

(1795-1821) John Keats

(1796-1863) Bocage

(1797-1851) Mary Wollestonecraft Shelley

(1797-1851) Mrs. Frances Trollope

(1797-1856) Heinrich Heine

(1797-1856) Madame Vestris

(1799-1850) Honore de Balzac
(1802-1870) Alexandre Dumas, pere
(1802-1876) Harriet Martineau
(1802-1885) Victor Hugo
(1803-1873) Edward George Bulwer-Lyton
(1803-1882) Ralph Waldo Emerson
(1804-1864) Nathaniel Hawthorne
(1804-1876) George Sand
(1804-1878) Samuel Phelps
(1806-1861) Elizabeth Barett Browning
(1806-1872) Edwin Forrest
(1807-1882) Henry Wadsworth Longfellow
(1807-1892) John Greenleaf Whittier
(1808-1860) Thomas D. "Jim Crow" Rice
(1809-1849) Edgar Allan Poe
(1809-1892) Alfred, Lord Tennyson
(1809-1893) Fanny Kemble
(1809-1894) Oliver Wendel Holmes
(1810-1891) P.T. Barnum
(1811-1863) William Makepeace Thackery
(1811-1896) Harriet Beecher Stowe
(1812-1870) Charles Dickens
(1812-1889) Robert Browning
(1815-1862) E.P. Christy
(1816-1855) Charlotte Bronte
(1816-1876) Charlotte Cushman
(1817-1862) Henry David Thoreau
(1818-1848) Emily Bronte
(1819-1880) George Eliot
(1819-1891) Herman Melville

(1819-1891) James Russell Lowell
(1819-1892) Walt Whitman
(1821-1858) Rachel
(1830-1886) Emily Dickens
(1832-1888) Louisa May Alcott